Divine Design For Liberated Living

A Tried and True Method for Success

Dr. Charles S. Lowery

Table of Contents

To my Dad and Mom who gave me the
Divine Design for my life.

The Choosy God

A first grader once said that he thought the First Commandment was when Eve told Adam to eat the apple. The Ten Commandments can be confusing. Life in America is confusing. What if you were watching a football game and each of the players had on a different uniform? The referees dressed in whatever attire they chose. The players wore whatever uniform they felt like wearing. Some of them were kicking, some were passing, and some were lying down. You would think that was crazy. Football was never intended to be played that way. Today in America we may think life is not as God intended. A national magazine said this about America's values: "We have a deep, vexing national anxiety about the nagging sense that unlimited personal freedom and rampaging materialism yield only greater hungers and lonelier nights." We are frantically searching for a value system.

The Ten Commandments, the words of God, offer a way out of this confusion. Isn't it great to know they are not words from philosophers, psychologists, or attorneys? That is why we can understand them. They are clear, simple words. In fact, there are only 286 words in the Ten Commandments. There are 30,000 words regulating lettuce in this country. There are approximately 35 million laws just to enforce these simple Ten Commandments.

The Bible refers to the Ten Commandments as the Law. When Jesus criticized the law in the New Testament, He was not talking about the Ten Commandments. Man had taken the Commandments and corrupted them. They had incorporated 611 nitpicking laws based on the Ten Commandments. They were so specific about the letter of the law that they forgot the spirit of the law. The Ten Commandments serve two functions. They are the primary guidelines that God has for His covenant people. In other words, they teach God's covenant people how to live. They also restrict evil in an unregenerate world. James Madison, the fourth President of the United States, said: "We have staked the whole future of American civilization not upon the power of the government, far from it. We have staked the future of all of our political institutions upon the capacity of each and every one of us to govern ourselves according to the Ten Commandments of God." Government does not work unless there is something else that governs the individual citizen. In a fallen world, we need boundaries and regulations.

Imagine what chaos there would be if there were no stoplights at busy intersections. People could be killed or hurt. At the very least they would be panicked, stressed out and confused. Sound familiar? The declining values in America have left the country in various states of instability, panic and dysfunction. Regulations are for all. If we do not kill, but allow others to kill, our society is in trouble. The Ten Commandments are the foundation, the building blocks, for society. Wouldn't America be better if you didn't have to lock your doors when you went to sleep, or left your house? What if you did not have to worry about violence? What if you could let your kids roam freely around your neighborhood? We would have a society in which we could all live. Boundaries are good. Railroad tracks do not restrict a train. They release a train to move faster. God gives us boundaries to protect, not restrict us. They release us to be what He created us to be. You might say that as Christians we are not under the law. You are right. We are not under the law. The law is our guideline for life. The gospel tells us what God has already done through Jesus Christ. He has fulfilled the law which we cannot fulfill.

The Old Testament has three kinds of laws: ceremonial law, civil law, and moral law. The ceremonial law was built around the sacrificial system and was a shadow of what was to come. It was a shadow of the Lamb of God who would be the ultimate sacrifice. Once Jesus came, there was no need for sacrifice. The civil law governed the nation of Israel, the nation from which the Messiah would come. God intervened and sent the Messiah. We do not live in a theocracy anymore. We do not need to be so involved with the civil law because one day Jesus Christ will come back and reign in a true theocracy. We also have the moral law which defines how we live daily with God and each other. The moral law runs throughout the New Testament because God has written it on our hearts. It is not only in His Word. His power in us gives us a "desire" to follow His moral law.

In studying the Bible, understand two things. First, there are specific commands that speak directly to us. For example, Paul wrote a letter to the Ephesians, the church at Ephesus. He spoke directly to them. He is also speaking to us. Second, for the elements that are not specific, we look for principles that apply. For example, in Habakkuk, the Israelites were concerned that the Babylonians would destroy them. God taught them not to be afraid of the Babylonians but to trust Him. We cannot apply the specifics to our situation, but the principle in Habakkuk is that God can protect us. Consider the principles within their context. Use common sense. God told Peter to walk on the water. Does that mean every time you walk by a lake you should want to walk on water because that is what God told us to do? I suggest not. That was a specific command to a specific person at a specific time.

Look at Exodus 19:3-6: "Moses went up to God, and the Lord

called to him from the mountain, saying, 'Thus you shall say to the house of Jacob, and tell the children of Israel: "You have seen what I did to the Egyptians, and how I bore you on eagles' wings and brought you to Myself. Now therefore, if you will indeed obey My voice and keep My covenant, then you shall be a special treasure to Me above all people; for all the earth is Mine. And you shall be to Me a kingdom of priests and a holy nation.'" These are the words which you shall speak to the children of Israel." God tells Moses that before he gives the Israelites the Ten Commandments, he is to remind them of what God has done for them. Grace is not only a New Testament concept, grace is throughout the Bible. Moses is to tell the children of Israel that once they were not a people and now they are God's people. Once they were in bondage and now they are free. Once they were in Egypt, and now they are in the Promised Land. These commandments are not rules and regulations for them to follow in order to be chosen by God. They have already been chosen and redeemed by God. The commandments are given to these redeemed people as a way to live. They were established to protect them for the best life possible in the Promised Land He gave them. The Ten Commandments are actually called the Ten Words. Jesus referred to them as the Commandments, but in the Old Testament, they were called the Ten Words. The Bible says they were spoken by God, and Exodus 31 says they were written with God's finger. He wrote the Ten Commandments on the tablets of stone with His finger. They are negative in form but positive in application because they are meant for redeemed people. God shows a redeemed people how to live once He has taken them out of bondage and given them the Promised Land.

The Old Testament and New Testament have parallel themes. In the Old Testament, the Israelites escaped from slavery in Egypt by putting the blood of the Passover lamb on their door frames. The angel of death—the last plague—passed over their houses sparing their firstborn and they escaped. Once released from bondage, they were given the law. In the New Testament, Jesus observed the Passover the night before He died. What He was telling the people was that He is the Lamb of God. He is the Passover Lamb. He is the way to redemption. They were taken out of slavery. You will be taken out of sin and slavery. How? By the Passover Lamb. He is God's ultimate sacrifice. Pentecost has similar parallels in the Old and New Testaments. In the Old Testament at Pentecost the Israelites received the law from Moses. For Christians, Pentecost is when God sends the Holy Spirit into our lives, when the law is written upon our heart. We now have Him within us which gives us power for a life different life from the natural life. Grace permeates the Old Testament and New Testament. By grace, God redeems mankind. He then teaches us how to live.

In Exodus 20:3 we have the First Commandment: "You shall have no other gods before Me." Isaiah 44:6 says it beautifully, "Thus says the Lord, the King of Israel, and his Redeemer, the Lord of hosts: I am the First and I am the Last; besides Me there is no God." Because He has redeemed you, He wants you to look to Him for everything. He does not want you to be dependent on anyone or anything else. He wants you to be dependent on Him for every good thing you need in this world, and He wants you to depend on Him to take you through the hard times. He wants you to choose Him as your one true God. There comes a time when each of us has to settle the affection of our hearts and the authority of our lives. Who is going to guide us and lead us?

Mark 12:29-30 says, "Jesus answered him, 'The first of all the commandments is: Hear, O Israel, the Lord our God, the Lord is one. And you shall love the Lord your God with all your heart, with all your soul, with all your mind, and with all your strength.' This is the first commandment." The teachers of the law were testing Him. They asked, "What about these commandments?"

Jesus answered that you can sum up the commandments — not all of those 611 nitpicking rules man made — but the Ten Commandments that God wrote, this way. First is that you love the Lord your God with all of your heart, with all of your mind, and all of your soul. Second is that you love your neighbor as yourself. The first four Commandments tell us how to relate to God, and the next six Commandments tell us how to relate to each other. What Jesus is saying is that if you get your relationship right with God, relationships with others will fall into place. If you love your neighbor, you won't take his life, you won't steal his wife, and you won't lie about him. You will be the kind of person God wants you to be.

How can I settle the affection of my heart? How can I settle the authority of my life? In John 5:39 Jesus says, "You search the Scriptures, for in them you think you have eternal life; and these are they which testify of me. But you are not willing to come to Me that you may have life." Jesus says that you have turned the principles of God into a moral code, into a philosophy of do's and don'ts. These laws do not offer life but death. The way to understand the commandments of God is to know the law giver. This affection of the heart has to be settled with the Person, not with a philosophy. The law does not measure up. The law allows us to see that we cannot keep the Ten Commandments. We all fall short and do not measure up. The Ten Commandments cannot do what Jesus does. The law cannot set you free, the law cannot forgive you your sins, the law cannot justify you, and the law cannot give you the power on the inside to be what God created you to be. Observing the Ten Commandments gives you a better way to live, even if you are not a Christian, but Jesus gives you the only way to eternal life.

Jesus is saying the difference is the connection. The commandments have to be connected to a Person. Let's say you go to the hardware store and there is a sprinkler head for $2.20. On the shelf, the sprinkler head is worthless, but if you connect it to a waterline, this sprinkler head is very valuable. It can bring life and beauty to flowers and shrubs. It has incredible value if it is connected to a waterline. The Ten Commandments are of no value unless you are connected to Jesus Christ. He is the connection to life. He put the law in your heart. He gives you the power to be what He created you to be. The First Commandment is not only a command, it is a promise. He is the sovereign God who spoke and created life. He loves you enough to choose you. He redeemed you. He is the one Who can get you out of your mess and He desires to help. He is the one Who loves you unconditionally. He has chosen you. All God asks in His First Commandment is that we choose Him back—that we choose Him as our one true God.

I am a big Dallas Cowboys fan. I am actually on the team. I have the hat and the jersey. I am a Dallas Cowboy. I do not know if you have seen me play, but I am on the team. You say, "Now wait a minute. I don't know if you're a Cowboy or not. You have too much gut for a Cowboy. I'm not sure you're a Cowboy. Tell you what, I think I'll go ask the coach if you're a Dallas Cowboy." I then become a little nervous because I know that I am really not a Dallas Cowboy. I have the hat and the jersey, and I do watch them every week, but I am not really a Cowboy. When you ask the coach about Charles Lowery, he will say "Who?" "Charles Lowery, do you know him?" "Nah. I don't know him." God says He has a team. His team is chosen by the coach—God Himself. You are a first round draft choice. The price is Jesus Christ. You've been chosen to be on the team. After being chosen, you have to decide that the affection of your heart is set on Jesus Christ. Only you and the coach know if you are on the team.

Some of you go to church every Sunday. You are there every week, and you look like everyone else, but deep down inside you know you are not on the team. You wear the hat and you have the outfit, but you know that you haven't set your affection on Christ the Lord. You have not trusted in Him for eternal life. Today you need to make that decision to accept Christ personally. Be on God's team, don't just look like it, but be on the team. Once you're on the team, the Commandments make sense. If you're not a Dallas Cowboy and you happen to be in Dallas and the Cowboys are doing wind sprints, you won't want to do wind sprints too because you're not on the team. You are in Dallas to go to Nordstrom's. Wind sprints have no purpose. Why do they have all those plays? The Cowboys understand because they are on the team. The Commandments will never make sense to you unless you're on the team, unless you're connected to the coach. Jesus says there will be people who thought they were on the team. They had the hat. They had the jacket. But Jesus said, "I do not know you. Depart from me. I never knew you. You weren't on the team. Oh, you came every week to the games, but you weren't on the team."

I'd like all of us to settle the affection of our heart, the authority of our lives. If you believe in Jesus Christ, the curse of sin, which is death, is no longer on you. You have eternal life. That is being a Christ follower. Obey Christ because the consequence of sin is pain, and by obeying Christ, you can alleviate much pain in this world. That's what God's Commandments are. He has the keys to life, but you have to have the connection and you have to be on His team.

Focus on what God would have you do. I don't know where you are, but I know that God chose you. He wants goodness and mercy to follow you all the days of your life. You may be a Christian — you believe in Christ — but you're in pain. Sometimes that is because you run your life. You make those decisions. God's not the authority in your life. You don't look to Him. The result is pain. Decide now to give Him control of your life. Or maybe you never made that decision to be on God's team. You don't want to be an outsider. You want a connection with Jesus Christ. Decide now to ask Him into your heart and life. Receive Him now as your Savior from sin and death.

Image Is Everything

In our society image is important. The Second Commandment tells us not to create an image because you cannot represent God. You may think the Second Commandment does not apply to you. You may say, "Charles, look, I'm not making any images. I flunked ceramics. I didn't do well in shop, either. I don't make graven images. That's one commandment that I don't violate." The First Commandment says not to worship a false God. The Second Commandment says not to worship the true God in a false way, which is the essence of idolatry.

We find the Second Commandment in Exodus 20:4-6, "You shall not make for yourself a carved image — any likeness of anything that is in heaven above, or that is in the earth beneath, or that is in the water under the earth; you shall not bow down to them nor serve them. For I, the Lord your God, am a jealous God, visiting the iniquity of the fathers upon the children to the third and fourth generations of those who hate Me, but showing mercy to thousands of those who love Me and keep My commandments." Why would God be jealous? "Jealous" here does not mean envious, but rather to be aggressive towards righteousness. He is jealous for our sake. He wants us to have the best. He does not want us to settle for a substitution, a shadow. Verse 5 says that if we have the wrong image of God, not only will we suffer, but the next generation will suffer and even the generation after that will suffer. But, He says He will continue to bless those who love Him. God is saying that if a generation does not put Him in His rightful place, it will replace Him with other things, and those things will affect the following generations. Why would God give us this commandment? Why would He tell us not to have images? God knows us because He made us and knew it would be very hard for us to worship an invisible God. How can you have a personal relationship with someone that's invisible? The Israelites' neighbors had foreign gods that they could look at and hold. God knew that we would be tempted like they were and want something to hold, something that would represent God, a reminder. But what God is telling us is that anything we do to represent Him will reduce Him. It's like trying to represent Mount Rushmore with silly putty. It does not work.

God is not talking about art. There were art objects in the tabernacle. He is talking about giving power to symbols. Symbols become the focal point of our connection to God. He wants Jesus to be the only focal point and connection. Take, for example, something that's common in our society, the crucifix. J. I. Packard says, "The crucifix highlights Jesus' human weakness without conveying His divine strength." You see Jesus' pain and suffering, but you do not see His victory. You see a dying Jesus, but you don't see a living Jesus. It's not what the crucifix says, it's what it doesn't say. Why not use an empty tomb? Why not use a manger? Nothing will represent God because it cannot encompass the totality of God. If we do not have a conscious awareness of the presence of God in our lives, then we want something to give us an awareness of God. It is a sign that we are spiritually stagnant when we look for other ways to contact God. We look for the tangible to reach the intangible.

Psalm 115:3-8 says, "But our God is in heaven; He does whatever He pleases. Their idols are silver and gold, the work of men's hands. They have mouths, but they do not speak; Eyes they have, but they do not see; They have ears, but they do not hear; Noses they have, but they do not smell; They have hands, but they do not handle; Feet they have, but they do not walk; Nor do they mutter through their throat. Those who make them are like them; So is everyone who trusts in them." Isaiah 44:19: "And no one considers in his heart, Nor is there knowledge nor understanding to say, 'I have burned half of it in the fire, Yes, I have also baked bread on its coals; I have roasted meat and eaten it; And shall I make the rest of it an abomination? Shall I fall down before a block of wood?" God is saying we should not worship what we create with our own hands. Can you eat half and worship the rest? Idols are no good, they are dead. Do not settle for a substitute. That idol will not feed you when you are in your wilderness. That idol will not lead you when you do not know where to go. That idol will always let you down. Don't waste your worship.

Kids love to play in the church when the worship service is over. Sometimes mothers admonish them telling them to straighten up and not run in church. This is God's house. Kids look around wondering where He is, they sure didn't see Him. The church is not God's house. The Bible says very clearly that we are God's house. When we make a symbol of this building, God wants us to be careful.

A pastor said, "In our church we shake hands with visitors each Sunday morning. When it was omitted one Sunday, someone commented, 'I just don't feel as if I've been to church today." I've heard that often. If we change a part of the service, people say, "Well, Pastor, it just didn't feel like church." Be careful, because the Second Commandment says you are very close to making something besides Jesus your connection to God. If you don't understand that illustration, just remember the words of that country song, "I don't care if it rains or freezes, as long as I have my plastic Jesus," — something to look at, something to hold on to. Images mislead man and dishonor God.

Romans 1:21-23 says, "Because, although they knew God, they did not glorify Him as God, nor were thankful, but became futile in their thoughts, and their foolish hearts were darkened. Professing to be wise, they became fools, and changed the glory of the incorruptible God into an image made like corruptible man, and birds, and four-footed animals, and creeping things." Fashioning an idol is an attempt to reduce God down to size, to make God in our image, to make Him manageable. Image is everything. Are you making any images? You probably are not making any physical images, but what about mental images? What is your image of God? Is it based on your imagination, or is it based on revelation from His book? Is it based on what your mom and dad taught you, or is it based on what God taught you? Is it based on a negative feeling from an authority figure, or does it come from what God tells you about Himself?

Some imagine God as a tightfisted judge, telling you that you are guilty, or a military general giving you orders but never listening. Some imagine God as a mechanic: I call him Mr. Goodwrench God, always there to fix things when you mess up. Many think of God as the Grandpa-George Burns-kind-of-guy. Grandpa God is smoking a cigar and anything goes. Whatever you want to do is fine with him. Some people think God is a celestial Santa Claus. Ask Him and He will give you whatever you want. God says whenever you fashion Him by your imagination rather than His revelation through His Word, you have made an idol. You have made a false god because God tells you what He is like in His Word. In the Bible, God is described as a father who loves you and doesn't want you to get hurt. He tells you the things that can cause you pain and even disciplines you so you will not be hurt again. God is described in many ways. He is a nursing mother who wants to love you and spend time with you, a shepherd looking for a lost sheep, and a just judge who one day will rule with truth and justice. God has provided many images, but the images come from His Book, not your imagination.

Most of us would agree that our society is in trouble. Why is that? The problem is not with the First Commandment (you are not to have any other gods) but with the Second Commandment. It is not that we join another religion. It is that we reshape our religion. We want to re-imagine God. We want to change things to make God politically correct. We want to be a Christian and stay in the church, but maybe deny the Trinity. We may say Jesus didn't really come back from the dead, or that He is not really the way to inherit eternal life. His blood isn't really necessary for salvation. We do not want the truth but we do not want to leave the church. We want to be Christian, but we want to manage God. We want to tell Him what we want to do, and then we want Him to honor us.

Groups often send me letters. These groups even make threats telling me that what they do is right even though God says it is wrong. They want me to re-imagine God and accept their beliefs. Is that new? Nothing is new. When God gave this commandment, the Israelites were making a graven image. Exodus 32 says, "When the people saw that Moses delayed coming down from the mountain, the people gathered together to Aaron, and said to him, 'Come, make us gods that shall go before us." Come; make us a god we can push around. Oh, we want God. We want His power, but we want to manipulate Him. Why would the Israelites want Aaron involved in creating images? They want the good housekeeping seal of approval. They want Aaron, a priest, to say it's OK. They want a seminary professor to say it's OK. They want their pastor to say it's OK. They want the seal of approval so that they can live the way they want.

When you say you do not need Jesus' cross or His blood in

order to be right with God—that all you need is to contact that god inside you—you reject the only way that God says will get you into His heaven. You refuse the only way that God gives to remove your sin. When you reject God's commandments for your sexuality and instead re-imagine God to suit the most corrupt and perverted instincts, then you are in serious trouble. We as a society are in serious trouble, and not only are we in trouble, our children are in trouble and their children's children are in trouble. God doesn't want you to create a false god, not because He's so jealous but because He doesn't want you to destroy your life. He doesn't want you to destroy society. Not only that, He doesn't want your kids to live with the repercussions and ramifications of your deciding to be your own god. God says this out of love. God is to be the God that's revealed to us in the Scripture, the one true God.

Colossians 1:26-27 says, "The mystery which has been hidden from ages and from generations, but now has been revealed to His saints. To them God willed to make known what are the riches of the glory of this mystery among the Gentiles." What is that mystery? What is the image that you are chasing? People who make idols are homesick for the one true God. When people look to something else, they do not have the conscious awareness, the presence, of God in their life. The mystery is that Christ, the hope of glory, is in you. The only image God wants you to have is the image of Jesus Christ. He is the invisible God made visible. Why was Jesus born so many years ago? I used to think, "You know, God, You didn't think this through. If CNN were around, it would have been a whole lot easier to get the word out." There are no photographs of Jesus Christ. As a matter of fact, the only physical description of Jesus says He was not good looking. We are not talking about a physical image, we are talking about a spiritual image. Jesus is the character of God, Jesus is the Spirit of God. We do not need the visible. What we need is an invisible means of support. We need to feel the presence of Jesus in our life. He is our hope. He is our glory, and when you have a personal Jesus, you don't need a plastic Jesus.

Christian Herder, the Governor of Massachusetts, was running for a second term and had a busy schedule. He hadn't had time for breakfast or lunch and was famished by the time he went to a church barbecue. As he progressed through the line, a woman placed a small piece of chicken on his plate. "Excuse me," Governor Herder said, "Do you mind if I have another piece of chicken?" "Sorry," the woman replied, "I'm only supposed to give one piece to each person. You have your piece." The Governor was not a proud man, but he was very hungry. So, he decided to throw a little weight around. He said, "Lady, do you know who I am? I'm the Governor of the State." She said, "Sir, do you know who I am? I'm the lady in charge of the chicken." God says in the kindest way He can say it. He's in charge of the chicken. He's in charge of eternal life. He's in charge of the universe. You are the creation, He is the Creator, and the only view He wants you to have of Him is through Jesus Christ. The only contact you are to have is through Jesus. Otherwise, you're going to have a poor substitute, you're going to settle for the shadow. The Bible says that Jesus is the only view God wants you to have. You may think one person's view of God is just as valid as another person's view of God. The Bible says you're wrong. There's only one view of God, and that comes from His Word from the invisible becoming visible in Jesus Christ. God says if that's not your view, not only are you in trouble, not only is society in trouble, but your children and their children are in trouble. We all need an invisible means of support, and idol worship is a meager means to cure your homesickness for the one true God.

A little boy was flying a kite that reached into the clouds, so he couldn't really see it. A man asked him what he was doing. He said, "Flying a kite." The man said, "But you can't see the kite."

The boy said, "No, I know I can't see the kite." He said, "Well, how do you know it's up there?" The boy said, "Every now and then I feel a tug on the string." No one has ever seen God, but He tugs on your heart. Every now and then He'll give you a jolt from His Word. He is the God of the Bible, and He is revealed through His Son, Jesus Christ.

When you think of God, what is He like? Is He the God of the Bible, or is He the God of your imagination or re-imagination? Have you ever accepted Christ and His death for your sins? Are you buying what society says: that one person's view of God is as good as another's? God's Word tells us that is wrong. He gives eternal life, and you get it through Jesus. Or maybe you've accepted Christ, but have started looking for symbols. You go to church as if visiting a rich relative once a week; you leave God there and return to a life of emptiness. Maybe you need to rededicate your life and say, "I want the one true God. I don't want to settle for substitutes. I want someone who can feed me in my wilderness. I want someone who can lead me when I am misdirected." That God is the One True God, revealed in the Bible and made visible in Jesus Christ.

"Don't Take My Name Lightly"

Historically one's name had more meaning than it does today. We don't take names seriously. After the Civil War, a group of wealthy businessmen approached Robert E. Lee and said, "We're going to start an insurance company, and we want you to be the president. You won't have to do anything. We'll pay you a comfortable salary if you'll just be president of the company." Robert E. Lee discovered that they really just wanted to use his name. This is what he replied: "Gentlemen, I have nothing left but my name, and that is not for sale." He understood that there is a power and a reputation that goes with a name. Even in our day a name is important. For 28 years an escaped convict was able to stay free because he used an assumed name. In April 1989 he turned himself in. When they asked him why, Sylvan Carter said, "I wanted to have my own name on my tombstone." In other words, I'm tired of living a lie. When I die I want to make sure I'm the one who dies.

The Third Commandment concerns His names. Exodus 20:7 says, "You shall not take the name of the Lord your God in vain, for the Lord will not hold him guiltless who takes His name in vain." In Exodus 3:15 God says to Moses, "Thus you shall say to the children of Israel: The Lord God of your fathers, the God of Abraham, the God of Isaac, the God of Jacob, has sent me to you. This is My name forever, and this is My memorial to all generations." In the Old Testament, name and essence were intertwined. The first four commandments talk about worship. Part of worship is understanding and revering the name of God. The name of God reveals the character of God. In the Old Testament, they were so careful about the name of God that they would not even pronounce it. When scribes copied the Scriptures and came to the name of God, they stopped, fasted and prayed, and wrote the name of God with a new quill. He'd use the old one to finish the rest of the text. The name of God was spoken once, and only by the high priest when he entered the holy of holies. They revered the name of God because using a person's name implied his power and reputation. We do that today. We may use someone's name on our resume because of that person's reputation. God says He does not want us to use His name lightly. Be careful of every word you say. Especially be careful with the words you say regarding His name.

Graffiti—defacing property by painting words on it—is a modern-day illustration of the importance of words. Sociologists, community leaders, and law enforcement officials say that areas that tolerate graffiti and the defacing of property are areas where a general sense of pride in the community is down and the crime rate is up. You may say, "Well it's only words," but if we don't care about the words we use, we don't care about the kind of people we are and how we relate to others. What graffiti says is if you take this part of your life lightly, you take every other part of your life lightly. The mouth that takes God's name lightly reflects a heart that takes God lightly. Who we are and what we think comes is expressed in what we speak. Graffiti shows contempt for property, for others, and for ourselves; it's an outer symptom of an inner problem. Taking God's name lightly is an outer expression of an inner attitude.

Jesus says we can tell much about what's inside a person by the words he speaks. In Matthew 12:34, 37 He says, "For out of the abundance of the heart the mouth speaks .... For by your words you will be justified, and by your words you will be condemned." We might express it as "What's in the well comes out in the bucket." What God tells us in the Third Commandment is to treat His name with reverence. In Old Testament times there were no credit reports and credit bureaus, so they made an oath. If someone asked, "How do I know you will pay this back?" they'd say, "I will give an oath to God—as the Lord liveth, I will pay this back." In other words, "If I don't pay this back, may God strike me." Some people, after making that oath, didn't keep their promises. They took the consequence out of the Lord's name and thereby dishonored it. God tells us to be very careful of the words we choose and especially of the words that relate to Him. Don't blaspheme the name of the Lord. Don't make fun of the name of the Lord. That means don't use it carelessly or curse with it. Don't damn someone by using the name of God, and don't tell somebody to go to hell using the name of God. Only God has the ability to damn people or send people to hell.

When you say, "God revealed this to me" to achieve your own agenda, you're taking the name of the Lord lightly. Last week I preached at the New Heritage USA. Radisson Hotels bought the hotel complex where Jim Bakker had his Heritage USA years ago. I walked around the sprawling campus and came upon a huge building with a crane still there. It occurred to me that it was a memorial to someone who used God's name in vain, who used God for his own agenda, who literally got too big for his britches. Don't use religious talk that alienates people. If we're not careful, we use so much religious talk that people don't understand us.

They take God lightly because they think we are weird. A little boy killed a frog. He came into the house holding it up in the air and said, "Mama, look. I killed it. I beat it to death. I stomped on it. I knocked it against the wall." Then he saw the preacher there. He paused and added, "And then the Lord called it home." That's religious talk. You are trying to make yourself look more spiritual than everyone else. That also brings dishonor to His name. You make a promise in a marriage that you will honor God by cherishing this person. You then take it lightly when you don't follow through with that commitment. The word "vanity" occurs often in the Old Testament. It means to empty of content, to make God irrelevant. If God is irrelevant in your everyday life, if He means nothing to you once you walk out of church, you are taking the name of the Lord in vain. If we as a church become irrelevant to society, then we take the name of the Lord in vain. We take away the consequences of His name when we fail to make God relevant to our world.

How else do we do that? Psalm 29:2 says, "Give unto the Lord the glory due to His name; worship the Lord in the beauty of holiness." As we move to the New Testament, we see not only words emphasized but our lives emphasized as well. 2 Timothy 2:19 says, "Nevertheless the solid foundation of God stands, having this seal: 'The Lord knows those who are His,' and 'Let everyone who names the name of Christ depart from iniquity.' But in a great house there are not only vessels of gold and silver, but also of wood and clay, some for honor and some for dishonor." In a big church there will be some people who live a life that honors God and others who live a life that dishonors God. Hypocrisy is words without practice. Hypocrisy in the church is worse than profanity in the streets. Why? You have named the name of the Lord. We, as Christians, carry His name. In the Old Testament God's people were referred to as "people who named the name of the Lord." When we name that name, it stands for God's character, for God's integrity. When we dishonor that name, we dishonor Him.

A friend once told me he could get me a Rolex watch. I asked him, "How much is it going to cost me?" He said, "$49.95." I said, "You can't get a Rolex watch for that." He said, "It's not a genuine Rolex, but it has Rolex on it. Everyone will think you have a Rolex. Everyone will think you're much more successful than you really are." He was offering the name at a bargain price. You wouldn't get the quality of a Rolex, you'd just get the name. This lowers the standard, the reputation, of the Rolex name. God says not to take His name lightly. Don't put His name on something of poor quality. We have the ability to exalt or defame God's reputation. Some people never become a Christian because they've never met a Christian. Some people never become a Christian because they have met a Christian. God says not to disgrace or profane His name. We do that when we profess much and possess little. Don't say you're His and live like you're not. I call that the profanity of indifference. The profanity of mediocrity is giving our best for second-rate causes and then not giving our best for God. Churches are guilty of that. If there is no preparation and no planning and people show up and say, "We have a little time, let's see what we can do for God," they are giving mediocrity to God. I've preached in some churches where the lack of preparation is embarrassing. I'm ready to preach and somebody gets up and says, "I haven't had time to prepare this week, and I've never sung this song before, but maybe God will bless it." I want to say, "Goodness! Sit down! Let me have your time. I haven't been eating Twinkies and Ding Dongs and watching television all week. I've been preparing. If you haven't, just sit down!" We are not to take God's name lightly. We're to do the best for Him. Whatever we do, we do it for His glory.

Philippians 2:9 says, "Therefore God also has highly exalted Him and given Him the name which is above every name." And Romans 10:13 says, "For whoever calls on the name of the Lord shall be saved." The name of the Lord is powerful; in fact, the name of Jesus Christ is very upsetting. You can take any other name to the government or school board and say, "I'd like to talk about this name." But if you say, "I'd like to talk about Jesus," it's very upsetting. Why? There is power in that name. The Bible says there's salvation in that name. The greatest blasphemy, really, is to claim to be a Christian and not know Christ. Reverence comes through personal knowledge. Sometimes when I'm preaching in the South, a man will come up to me after the service and say, "You know, I knew Fred Lowery. Isn't that your dad? You look a little bit like him, talk a little bit like him." That name brings reverence to me. We talk and give honor to what he did, what he stood for. There's honor there because it's personal. We know that name. The Bible says the only way to know God is through Jesus Christ. We are bound in covenant to God. First the covenant was in the Ten Commandments — the law — but Jesus came to fulfill that law, and now He makes a covenant with us. He is obligated to us because of His name. He tells us that if we will call upon His name, if you claim His name, He is obligated to give you salvation. He is obligated to save you not because you're good, but because He is good, because His name is good, because His character is good. There is only one name by which you can be saved, and that's the name of Jesus Christ.

Many people would say, "Oh, taking God's name lightly is not as important as God says it is." Let me give you an idea of the way we talk in America. The singer Tina Turner says, "I'm a Buddhist Baptist. My training is Baptist, and I can still relate to the Ten Commandments and the Ten Worlds. It's all very close as long as you contact the subconscious mind. That's where the coin of the Almighty is. I don't care what they feel about me and my tight pants on stage and my lips and my hair. I'm a chanter, and everyone who knows anything about chanting knows you correct everything in your life by chanting everyday." Tina keeps the Buddhist shrine in her house and says that praying and chanting every morning and evening was her path to salvation. God says, "Tina Turner, you have taken My name lightly, and I will not hold you guiltless." With all respect to Tina Turner, chanting "Nammyohorengekyo" will not get her into Heaven; only the name of Jesus Christ will do that. She has taken that name lightly. You say, "Oh, that's Tina Turner. That's that Hollywood crowd, that's not us." George Gallup did a survey of average Americans. He said, "Religion in America is very popular these days, but it is also very superficial. It does not change people's lives to the extent one would expect with the level of expressed faith. There is not much difference in the ethical behavior of Christians and non-Christians." He says that half of Christianity — those who call themselves Christians — don't know who delivered the Sermon on the Mount. Only ten percent appeared to possess transforming faith. That's people who say they're Christians. Fifteen percent who say they're Christians read the Bible daily. One-fourth of the people who say they're Christians never read the Bible. God says that there will be many people who call Him Lord, but they never knew Him. The Third Commandment tells us there is power in the name of the Lord, so don't take it lightly.

I was audited by the IRS when I was in graduate school and was scared to death. I went to the IRS office and waited my turn to talk to the IRS agent. The guy was a jerk. I don't know how else to say it. To everything I would say, he replied, "That's not right. You're lying." We had a neighbor providing child care at the time. He said, "That's not your neighbor, that's your sister or your mother. You can't deduct that." He was calling me a liar. I was getting, as King James would say, wrought. I was thinking, "I've had it with this guy." He sat there and belittled me. I started praying because I knew I was getting mad. I was thinking, "God, I am about to punch this guy's lights out. If I do, it's going to look bad. I mean, it's going to look bad for me, but it's going to look bad for You too. You know the liberal press: on the front page of the paper they'll put, 'Christian psychologist kills IRS man.' God, you've got to do something." I looked on this guy's desk. There, in the corner, was a small picture of Jesus. I said, "Excuse me, sir. May I ask you a question?" He said, "What?" I said, "Who's that?" I put my finger right on Jesus and smiled at the IRS man. He looked at me. He looked at that picture, and he dropped his head. I said again, "Who is that?" He said, "That's, that's ...." And he dropped his head again. He could not say the name Jesus. Why? Because he knew Jesus but he wasn't acting like Him and he knew that he was bringing dishonor to His name. Finally I said, "That's Jesus, isn't it?" That IRS man who had belittled me so much said, "Yes, sir. That's Jesus." His whole attitude changed. The whole interview changed. He was honest and still wouldn't allow a few deductions, but he wasn't ugly anymore. If you know Jesus and you're acting ugly and someone brings up His name, you will want to repent and act right.

How about you? Outside of your church attendance, are you bringing honor to the name of Jesus Christ? Was there a time when you knew that the only way you could be saved is by claiming the name of Jesus Christ? That you can't be saved by a religion or a routine, but only by trusting in His name, the name above all names? Have you mixed some worldly or New Age philosophy with Jesus? They don't mix. Don't take His name lightly. It is the Name above all names.

Faith, Family, Friends, and Fun

A group of Americans went on a big game hunt in Africa. They had African guides and made a lot of progress on the first and the second days. The third day they were so excited to get there that they were up early raring to go. The African guide said, "No, we're not going today." The Americans said, "What do you mean we're not going? We have to make time. We have to hurry." The guide said, "No, no, we've made a lot progress, but we're not going anywhere today. We're going to rest today. We're going to let our souls catch up with our bodies." It's very important to let your soul catch up with your body to make sure you're as successful spiritually as you are in other areas. If your life today is hectic, if your schedule allows no time for faith, family, friends, and fun, if you don't really have any time to pray or play, then your life is out of control.

Exodus 20:8 says, "Remember the Sabbath day, to keep it holy." The Fourth Commandment leads to the Fifth Commandment honor your father and mother because until you really understand the first four commandments about being right with God, it's very hard to be right with other people. After you are right with

God, then you "honor your father and mother, that your days may be long upon the land which the Lord your God has given you." The Fifth Commandment deals indirectly with God and the Fourth Commandment deals directly with God. If you deal with God directly, it's much easier to deal with people because you're still dealing with God indirectly. Everything we do, we do as unto the Lord. Notice that the Fifth Commandment is a commandment with a promise. It says that if you honor those in authority, it will go well with you. You will live long. I believe that's not only a promise to individuals, it's also a promise to the church and to society. If you honor those people whom God has put over you, you honor God. Our society is crumbling today because people have a hard time giving honor to those in authority over them. They want to do what they want to do when they want to do it. "Nobody tells me what to do." Our families are crumbling today because we have the same attitude: "Nobody tells me what to do. I do what I want to do." God says that if you operate that way, you won't live long—neither you nor your family nor your society.

Ephesians 6:1-4 says, "Children, obey your parents in the Lord, for this is right." And all the parents said, "Amen." Mark Twain said it best: "At 14, I was amazed at how stupid my daddy was, and at 21, I was amazed at how smart he had gotten in those seven years." We obey parents, not because we think they're right all the time, but we obey in the Lord, because we know God will take care of us and honor us as we honor our parents. And you, fathers, do not provoke your children to wrath. Updated version, don't drive your kids nuts. Relax a little bit. Don't pick about everything. Then it says, "But bring them up in the training and admonition of the Lord."

Let's look now at the Fourth Commandment. How was the Sabbath established? In Deuteronomy God tells the Israelites they are to have this Sabbath day because He has taken them out of slavery. He wants them to enjoy some rest. He wants them to have a time when they can relax and reflect on how good God was to them. He wants them to have a time of rest. Whatever God gives is good. Sometimes men and women take what is good and make it not good. What was meant to be joyful became a grim ritual. What was meant to be a day to enjoy became a day to endure. It became more regulation than celebration.

The Pharisees took what was good and kept adding to it and didn't know when to stop. They took the Sabbath and added regulations. For example, if a flea were to land on you on the Sabbath, you couldn't kill the flea. You could shoo it off, but you couldn't kill it because that would be hunting on the Sabbath. You couldn't travel far from your house on the Sabbath. But if you took a rope along the distance from your house, that was considered extending your house. So they laid out rope after rope after rope along the distance they wanted to travel on the Sabbath. They'd find loopholes to get around man-made laws. There was a ritual washing that occurred before the meal. It was good. They cleaned before they ate. Man said that if washing before the meal is good, then washing after the meal is good and instituted the ritual washing after the meal. They were very specific about how to wash. They had to have one and a half eggshells full of water, pour it down their hands and it had to drip all the way to the wrists or else they weren't clean. People living in the desert, poor people, had to store ritually clean water so they could dump it in eggshells and run it down their hands. That was supposed to draw them closer to God. When it had evolved to that, thank goodness Jesus showed up.

He said He was here to free them from all that, to take them out of that bondage, and to help them understand what it really means to be blessed. He came to remove regulation and give celebration.

In Mark 2:27-28 Jesus says, "The Sabbath was made for man,

and not man for the Sabbath. Therefore the Son of Man is also Lord of the Sabbath." Jesus and the Pharisees clashed because He broke their rules for the Sabbath. Jesus said that the Sabbath was made for man to enjoy. Paul takes that same theme in Galatians 4:10: "You observe days and months and seasons and years. I am afraid for you, lest I have labored for you in vain." Paul says you have this freedom. I have told you how Christ came to liberate you, and now you are returning to that same old ritual. He said he was afraid that he had labored in vain; afraid what he told them went in one ear and out the other.

In Colossians 2:16-17 Paul tells us that the Sabbath is part of the ceremonial law, which is not related to the moral law. "So let no one judge you in food or in drink, or regarding a festival or a new moon or Sabbaths, which are a shadow of things to come, but the substance is of Christ." Paul is saying the Sabbath is unique among the Ten Commandments. It's not stamped on human consciousness as a moral law. Rather, it's an ordinance. It's like circumcision. It has a symbolic meaning, and it was a shadow of what was to come. The Sabbath was a gift of God to the Jewish people, His special people, and it was a unique way to prepare them for the Messiah who was to come.

Remember there are three kinds of law: moral, civil, and ceremonial. The Ten Commandments are the moral law. They are reinstituted in a different way in the New Testament. Every commandment, except the Sabbath commandment, appears again in the New Testament. The Sabbath was essential in the Old Testament, but it was essential because God was preparing His people for the Messiah. God was showing them that what they now achieved by working, they would one day achieve by resting. When Jesus came He said his purpose was that your joy would be full, that you would understand and enjoy life. He and the disciples enjoyed life. They enjoyed life even on the Sabbath and it got them into big-time trouble. They had so much fun that the religious people accused them of being drunkards, wine imbibers, and gluttons. I hope that people say about me, "He has to drink more than Diet Coke. He's having too much fun." Jesus came to liberate us from that mentality. He said He came that you might have a little fun, that you may enjoy life. He came not to add more regulations but to celebrate. He came not to add burdens and sorrows but to relieve them. That is why they said, "Joy to the world, He is here."

Jesus shows a new way of looking at the Sabbath, a new way of looking at life. We can celebrate everyday. We can have quiet time with God wherever we are. God can enter our life wherever we are. You and I have a tendency to return to regulation from celebration. We have a tendency to return to laws that say you can't kill a flea, you can't start a fire, or you can't leave your house. They give us control. The Puritans went back to regulations. I read a story about a Puritan man who had been away at sea. He hadn't seen his wife in two years. The boat happened to return him home on the Sabbath, and his wife was waiting for him at the gate. He came up and kissed her. They threw him in jail for kissing his wife whom he hadn't seen for two years because he kissed her on the Sabbath. Can you imagine that? You see people's distorted view of God? You wonder why people don't come to church? It's because we have regulation rather than celebration.

Matthew 11:28 is what the Sabbath is all about now in our day: "Come to Me, all you who labor and are heavy laden, and I will give you rest. Take My yoke upon you and learn from Me, for I am gentle and lowly in heart, and you will find rest for your souls." The Sabbath was made for man, and men need the Sabbath. We don't need it in the way the Israelites in the Old Testament did, but we still need a time of rest. We need a time of reflection. We need time to regain our perspective about what's really important in life. There comes a time when you have to refocus. In the New

Testament, when the disciples were tired after the toils of ministry Jesus didn't say, "Hey guys, when the going gets tough, the tough get going. Just suck it up. We've got to go." He didn't say that. He took them away to the desert to rest, to be rejuvenated. The Sabbath is made for man because man needs the Sabbath. We need a time to slow down physically, emotionally, and spiritually.

The early church observed the Sabbath on the first day of the week because Christ was resurrected on the first day. It was logical to meet on the first day of the week, resurrection day. It is a good day to resurrect what God wants to do with you, to resurrect the dreams that He has put inside of you, to focus on what's important. Whether it is Saturday night or Sunday morning, take seriously that there's a time when you need to come together with God's people to refocus your life. It doesn't have to be solemn. You don't have to look like a donkey face all the time at church in order to take it seriously. You might say, "I don't have time to go to worship service." You don't have time not to. You will accomplish more by going to church every week than you ever dreamed you could on your own.

In the gold rush days, there were two groups of wagon trains headed for California. One group was lead by a Christian man, who decided that one day each week they would stop, worship God, rest, and rejuvenate. The other group decided that the best way to get there first was to never stop, never rest, just keep on going as far as they could go. They didn't rest at all, and, of course, the first ones to get to California were the first ones to get their names on the gold list, the first ones to get the gold. The wagon train that worshipped and rested on the Lord's Day arrived in California first even though both left the east at the same time. Rest is part of the natural rhythm of life. If you don't rest, although you're going fast, you will burn out, rust out, or bend over barking like a dog. You will be unable to do what God would have you do. We need a time of rest and relaxation. We need a time to focus on our faith, our family, our friends, and a time to have a little fun and enjoy life.

When we went to church when I was a kid, we'd get in the car and slam those doors. We were running late. Everyone's been hollering at each other. Then we would see the heathens outside in their yard. You know the heathens? Guy's out there in his undershirt drinking a Bud Light. They're playing softball. Man, they're laughing. They're running the bases. They're having fun. Then Dad says, "Look at all those heathens out there." He's trying to make a sermon out of the heathens. He doesn't know he's not making his point. "Look at those heathens." I'm going, "Yeah, yeah, I've been watching the heathens." Dad would mutter through his teeth, "They don't know the joy of Jesus, those heathens don't." I made a commitment in the backseat of my car when I was little, "I'm going to be a heathen when I grow up. They have all the fun."

Relax. Get up 30 minutes earlier than usual on Sunday. The devil tries to mess you up. I guarantee it. You can have everything laid out Saturday night, but the devil will come in at 2:00 in the morning and mess it all up. Get organized a little bit, and make it a priority that you're going to make Sunday a fun day, a special day. It will be good for you and your family. Sunday, when you worship, make sure you do activities that restore you, that renew you, that involve you in recreation. Remember, recreation means recreation. Have your soul and spirit involved in it. To not rest is a sign of immaturity. Who at your house doesn't want to rest? It's the little kids. You can't ever get kids to rest. Teenagers are immature. You can't get them to go to bed. You can't get them up, but you can't get them to go to bed. They don't understand they need that rest. And so God says, "Have a time set aside when you regain your perspective," remembering who God is, together with God's people; do it consistently.

Let's look at Matthew 11:28 again: "Come to Me, all you who labor and are heavy laden, and I will give you rest. Take My yoke upon you and learn from Me, for I am gentle and lowly in heart, and you will find rest for your souls." It tells us to come to a personality. Only Jesus can give you spiritual rest. You can play golf all weekend. You can sleep all weekend. You can sleep all week and still be tired because you're tired spiritually. You know that you're alienated from God. You know there are some relationship problems there, and only Jesus can give you rest from soul problems.

If Christianity is a burden for you, if church is a burden, somehow you have misunderstood and you have the wrong picture of God. You have somebody else's personality instead of Jesus' personality. You need to go back and read about who Christ is because you're living a life of regulation rather than celebration. God wants you to enjoy. The Bible says, "Let us go to the house of the Lord. I was glad when they said unto me, 'Let me go into the house of the Lord.'" That's the place where we can enjoy the eternal rest that God has given us. Jesus says, "My yoke is easy." Yoke means harness. You don't live a life without any kind of yoke, without any kind of harness. If you don't have Christ's harness, you have the world's harness, and the world's harness will wear you out. God says His harness is good for you. His harness may feel heavy at times, but it's like a scuba diver's gear. When it is in the water, it gives life. His harness is good for you.

You go to church every week for the same thing, to be reminded of what's important, to be reminded to focus, to get a different perspective on life rather than the world's harness, to be reminded that your faith is important, your family is important, your friends are important, that it's important to enjoy life, to slow down. I have a friend who said his dad hated traffic lights. Every time he'd come to a traffic light, he'd say he couldn't believe he had to stop and wait on everybody. He'd get stressed out. When he died, they had this funeral procession that headed down the street with the policeman out in front. They went right through all the traffic lights. His grandson got the biggest kick out of that. He said, "Look, look, granddaddy gets to go through them all. He's going to be so happy. He doesn't have to stop at any of them." Granddaddy is dead. He's not worried about traffic lights now. Even the traffic lights remind you to relax. If you spent time with the Lord at traffic lights, you'd have a pretty good time. Why are you in such a hurry, anyway? Where are you going? To meet God? If you're in such a big hurry, it would be a whole lot simpler to get to know Him now. Spend a little time with Him now.

What's the bottom line? Refocus. Decide to live in the rhythm that God has designed for you. Decide that you're going to be consistent in time with God and with God's people. It's a discipline, but the yoke is easy. Once you discipline yourself, you have the desire to do it. Discipline yourself and it becomes a delight. You enjoy it, and you have rest. When you have rest, let other people have rest. Get off their backs. Some of you think you are more biblical than the Bible. You put everyone on a guilt trip. Give them some rest too; they'll appreciate it. Some of you struggle with addictions. When do those addictions jump up and get you? They come when you're lonely, when you're angry, and when you're tired. That comes from not being in the rhythm of God's life, not spending time with Him and with His people. Jesus is the only one who can refresh your soul.

The Killer Instinct

The Sixth Commandment says, "Thou shall not commit murder." In a children's class the students were told that the commandment that had to do with their parents was, "Honor your father and your mother." Then they were asked what commandment had to do with their brothers and sisters. They responded in unison, "Thou shall not kill." We live in a violent society. It seems that animals have more protection than we do. If you don't believe that, let me share with you an AP report dated August 21, 1994. It says, "Hillside, New Jersey. Frank Bailen used a broom handle to kill a rat that was ravishing his garden. He thought he'd put an end to the situation by calling the Humane Society and asking them to remove the rat. He was wrong. The Humane Society issued two summonses against Mr. Bailen for killing the rat. The charges could have caused him to spend up to six months in jail and pay $1,250 in fines. Officials from the Humane Society pleaded in defense of rats' rights."

We live in a violent society whether you're a rat or a person. Even sports are violent. We have football, heavyweight boxing, and ice hockey. We watch murders on TV. Before a child is six years old, it's estimated that he has seen 6,000 murders on television. It's a violent and deadly society. In America today, 1 out of every 1,000 strangers that you encounter has murdered someone. Be careful of people you bump into in the grocery store.

We're not only killing each other, we're killing ourselves. Over the past three decades, the suicide rate among U. S. teens has more than tripled. You know that murder is wrong. You might have broken those other commandments, but not on this one. You think you can just sit back and relax because you don't commit murder. There are many different ways to commit murder; you just might have the killer instinct in you.

The Sixth Commandment is found in Exodus 20:13: "You shall not murder." Moses came down the mountain with the stone tablet. What's interesting is that Moses himself was a murderer. He had killed an overseer in the work camp. In those days life was very cheap. God knew that His people were going to be in difficult situations where life would be cheap. He knew that they would be around cultures that sacrificed babies to foreign gods. He wanted them to know that life was sacred, that people are not expendable, people are valuable. So He gives them the commandment, "You shall not murder." The King James Version says, "Thou shall not kill." Thou shall not murder is a more accurate translation because kill has other connotations. Lots of things are killed in the Bible. God even told His people to go to war. There were times when they would have to kill. God told them to kill certain animals and make them part of the sacrificial system. God told Noah that he could kill anything that lived and breathed for food. So you hunters don't have to worry. Jesus was a fisherman. He fished, and the fish had to be killed to be eaten.

It would be so much easier if things were cut and dry. This is right and this is wrong. But we live in a sinful world. Life is sacred, but because we live in a sinful world, decisions aren't always clear-cut. We find ourselves in situations in which we're forced not between right or wrong, but between two kinds of wrongs. We're forced to make a determination between two kinds of evil. The ethic doesn't change. Wrong is still wrong. Right is still right. But sometimes, one wrong may be less wrong than another wrong.

The Bible says, "Thou shall not murder." You should not take somebody's life just because you decide to, but there will be circumstances where you might have to make a choice. For example, let's say there's a guy with a gun in my house and he tells me that he's going to kill my family. What am I going to do? I already know that somebody will be murdered. Now the question is, who will be murdered? I am willing at that point in time to murder that person to keep him from murdering people I love. We call it war when we have many men committing murder. It gets tough in a sinful, fallen world. The Old Testament was similar. The Jewish interpretation of civil law was that the life of the mother was always a higher priority than the life of the unborn. If the question was not "will someone die" but "who will die," then the unborn was always to die rather than the mother. With capital punishment the state decides to kill someone. I believe that if someone commits murder, they should be put in prison for the rest of their life. What happens in our society, however, is we put them in jail with a life sentence but they are soon paroled. Often those people whom we put in jail get out and kill someone else. So the question then is not will somebody be murdered; it's who will be murdered. In that particular instance, I want the murderer to be murdered rather than you or me.

As technology advances, it will get more and more complicated. We'll have a person on life support systems who we're able to keep alive with technology, but it costs thousands of dollars a day. Who will make the decision to keep someone alive? It is very difficult. Baptists believe in the priesthood of the believer. We believe that we're all priests and we all go to God. We believe that the Holy Spirit lives within us and we have the ability to make individual decisions. You won't agree with some of my decisions, and I won't agree with some of yours. God will give each of us the guidance in those decisions.

1 John 3:11 says, "For this is the message that you heard from the beginning, that we should love one another, not as Cain who was of the wicked one and murdered his brother. And why did he murder him? Because his works were evil and his brother's righteous." God says that there can't be a clear-cut answer for every situation. There's no book you can look in that tells you on page 32, "When this happens, this is what to do." The Jewish people tried. They had over 600 laws, rules, and regulations, but they still couldn't cover everything. God gave us the Holy Spirit and the Word of God to guide us, but Jesus tells us the overriding principle is love. He says the message from the beginning is to love one another. When making those decisions, make them based on love.

I believe that war is never right, it's always wrong. Euthanasia is never right, it's always wrong. Capital punishment is never right, it's always wrong. Abortion is never right, it's always wrong. That's the ideal. That's where we say that love and truth should reign. But the fact is, although life is sacred, we live in a sinful world. And because we live in a sinful world, there will be honest physicians, committed lawmen, dedicated generals, sincere people like you and me who are put in situations where they have to choose not between right and wrong, but between two wrongs. They are put in horrible situations because we live in a horrible world. How are we to treat those people? We're to treat them as God treats us. In the Bible Cain, the wicked one, murdered his brother, and God's wrath burned against Cain. In one verse you see God's wrath but in the next verse you see God's grace. Even though His wrath came against Cain, His grace prevailed. He marked Cain with a mark to insure that no one else would kill him. He protected him. God's wrath comes, but God's grace also comes. We as a church and we as a people are to hold up the ideal. The Bible is a book of life. It's filled with the prescription for eternal life, the abundant life. It is the way to have a committed life. The Bible says that life is sacred. Life is not cheap. We also have to understand that God knows we are in a sinful world, and He sent His Son. If we're to interact with the sinners as Jesus did, we are to treat them as God treats us. Grace has to overcome wrath.

We can murder people in different ways. We can commit invisible murder. There is little difference between a dripping knife and a cutting tongue. It still hurts very much. Matthew 5:21 says, "You have heard that it was said to those of old, 'You shall not murder, and whoever murders will be in danger of the judgment.' But I say to you that whoever is angry with his brother without a cause shall be in danger of the judgment. And whoever says to his brother, 'Raca!' shall be in danger of the council. But whoever says, 'You fool!' shall be in danger of hell fire." We worry about getting caught and taken to court if we murder someone. There is another court. There is God's court. God not only knows what you do but what you think. God knows the motivation behind your action. God knows your heart and wants you to be sure you don't murder in your heart. He doesn't want your heart to become a headquarters for hate. You say, "Now wait a minute. If we merely think about murder, if we have hatred in our heart, we're in danger of hell fire?" What Jesus is saying is that we're all sinners that we all needed Him to die so we could go to Heaven rather than hell. We look at murder as a greater sin than harbored hate, but God says that it is the same.

In the Sermon on the Mount Jesus teaches that action begins with attitude. Cain "had an attitude" — his brother had something that he didn't have. He wanted his way. The main dimension of the killer instinct is anger. Whenever love is not in charge, whenever Jesus is not in charge, the killer instinct is. Hate grows, and we are like Cain. We say that we think someone got what I deserve.

At work maybe someone got the promotion that you wanted, or someone has a new house. You have hate in your heart. You think dark thoughts about that person, and you develop a killer instinct. It begins with attitude, advances to anger, and then anger is expressed in words. "That idiot didn't deserve the promotion. That stupid lady doesn't need a new house. She had everything she wanted in her old house." God will hold you responsible for those words. Cain asked, "Am I my brother's keeper?" The Bible clearly says that we are our brother's keeper; not only that, we are our brother's brother. We are to be concerned about the words and the labels we use.

If we label people "fool," we think it gives us a right to treat them differently. Labels remove the personality from the person and we attack a label. "That person is a fool. That person is an idiot." Jesus was labeled a blasphemer, and he died on the cross. We have to be careful because labels encourage the killer instinct not only in us but in those around us. For instance, we have some who would kill a person labeled an abortionist? They are labeled, and people think they can kill someone to keep them from killing other people. Is that God's way? That we would kill in order to protect because we label that person an abortionist. Other labels apply to that man as well—husband, father, he has a family. Let love guide you. Don't take matters into your own hands. Don't decide who's an idiot. Don't decide who's a blasphemer. Don't decide whom to kill. Let love guide you. Be angry about what's happening in this country, but have grace. Treat people the way you've been treated or else the killer instinct will take over.

The killer instinct says, "I matter more than you do. What I think is always right, and what you think is always wrong. I'm the center of the universe, and everything should revolve around me. If it doesn't, I'm going to label you. I'm going to talk about you, and I'm going to get what I deserve, and if I can't get it, I'm going to push you down to lift myself up." It's the killer instinct. It's in all of us. Someone put it this way, "Some men die in shrapnel and some men die in flames, but most men perish inch by inch playing their little games." You don't really murder anyone else with your words, you murder yourself. You destroy yourself inch by inch.

What's the cure? How do we go from that killer instinct to being what God would have us be? 1 John 3:14-15 says it this way, "We know that we have passed from death to life, because we love the brethren. He who does not love his brother abides in death. Whoever hates his brother is a murderer, and you know that no murderer has eternal life abiding in him." Hates his brother—have you ever hated anyone? The Bible says you're a murderer. We are all sinners. That's the whole idea. Verse 16 states, "By this we know love, because He laid down His life for us. And we also ought to lay down our lives for the brethren." You can gauge your relationship with God by your relationship with other people. You can gauge how you relate to God by how you relate to other people. You can gauge what you'd like to say to God by what you say to other people. So he says that the way to know you have love is when you lay down some things for your brother. Be willing to lay down that promotion. It's not God. It can't control your life. Be willing to lay down that new house. Don't let the killer instinct develop in you. Rejoice that someone else gets that house. Look at life from God's perspective. Lay down some things because the Christian life is not lived in the negative. You have to live in the positive. If you don't, you'll go back to the killer instinct.

Jesus told the story of the Good Samaritan. "Samaritan" was a very negative label. A Samaritan was part Jew and part Gentile. They were the outcasts. Jesus chose that label to show you labels don't matter; people matter. Religious people passed by a man who had been beaten, robbed, and left to die in a ditch. The Good Samaritan was willing to help him, and it cost. The killer instinct dies as you help other people, as you move out of yourself and ask, "What can I do? I can not criticize this world, not criticize my church, and not criticize the people in my church. What can I do to make this thing better?" Love lives. Love is the key to killing the killer instinct.

Let's get personal. What does this say to us? Have you put a knife in anyone's back lately? Have you talked about someone when you really didn't have the facts? You just babbled on. Many people tell me things and half of them are off the wall, untrue. When we put a knife in someone's back, we murder with our words. Some of you kids murder your parents with rebellious behavior. You kill your parents in slow motion as they watch what you do and how it affects your life. Some of you are murdering your marriage. You use negative, cutting words every day. If you keep using the same words week after week, you're on the verge of murdering your marriage. God wants you to use words of grace, not words of wrath.

A teacher in New York did an experiment in which she gave three ribbons to people in her class. One ribbon she wanted them to wear, and on the other two ribbons she wanted to put in gold letters, "You make a difference." She told them to wear this ribbon, and give the other ribbons to people who had made a difference in their lives. Tell them what a difference they've made in your life. One teenage boy went to a company to see a junior executive who had helped him on a project. He took his ribbon with him and said, "Look, I've been in class and this is my assignment. You helped me with my other project, and so, you came to mind. You have made a difference in my life. You encouraged me. Although I didn't do anything to deserve it, you helped me. I want you to have this ribbon. Not only that, I want to give you two ribbons and encourage you to do the same thing."

The junior executive took the ribbons and thanked the kid and thought, "That's kind of a corny project for teenagers. I'm a junior executive of a company. I shouldn't do things like that." But he kept looking at the ribbons. Finally he said, "You know, maybe I ought to do it." He went to his boss, the CEO of the company, and he said, "Look, this is kind of corny, but this teenager brought a ribbon to me and asked me to do the same thing. So I want to tell you that you've made a difference in my life. I didn't know anything but you hired me and gave me a chance. You've overlooked my mistakes, and I just want to give you this ribbon and tell you that you've made a difference in my life. Not only that, I'm going to give you two ribbons. I know it's kind of corny, but why don't you try this. It's added something to my life by doing it. It's amazing what positive words will do for your life."

The CEO looked at the ribbons and he thought, "This is corny." Here he is, the CEO of the company, and he's carrying ribbons around that say "You make a difference." He thought, "Well, you know, he asked me to do it and I ought to do it to somebody. I really don't feel comfortable doing it to anybody here at the company." His teenage son came to mind. He said, "You know, I ought to do something for him. I've never really done anything to express my love for him. I'll do that." So he went home and said, "Son, let me talk to you a minute. I know I give you a hard time. I know I holler about your grades, about the way you dress, your friends, and your hair. I know I holler about most everything. But look, I really do love you. I know I tend to speak negative words, but I want to tell you that I love you. I have this ribbon that says, 'You make a difference.' I want to give you this ribbon because you've made a difference in my life. The day you were born was the happiest day of my life. The reason I work so hard at the company is because I want you to have a good education. I do it for you. I love you so much. You've made a difference in my life." He wasn't prepared for what happened. All of a sudden, tears started coming out of the boy's eyes. He started to sob. The father put his arm around him and asked, "Are you OK, Son?" He said, "Yeah, Dad. I'm OK. It's been a very difficult year. Things just haven't gone right at all, and really, Dad, I thought that you were very disappointed in me. I thought you were ashamed of me. I've gotten so depressed about life. After supper tonight I planned to kill myself, but this ribbon has made the difference, and now I can go on." God tells us we will give an account of every idle word we speak. You can murder just as easily with words as you can with a gun or a knife.

Where does this take us? Let me give you an analogy. Murder may not seem like a good subject, but it's actually an encouraging subject. God used murder to save you and me. The essence of the gospel is the substitutionary death of Jesus for the sins of the world. It's one of the most violent acts known—the death, the murder, of God's Son on the cross. It was conceived in God's heart and committed to by Jesus. That decision had to be made, the decision between two choices that both looked bad. Either human beings had to suffer eternal death for their sins or Jesus, the Son of God, had to be crucified—murdered—for their sins so that they could have eternal life. God chose the life for us. God, because of His love, chose to lift us out of this sinful world and one day place us in His home called Heaven. Jesus Christ was murdered, but out of the murder came God's grace and God's love. You think about what that murder cost Him before you think about murdering somebody else.

Looking for Love

The Seventh Commandment involves a word that we all talk about in our society — sex. The Victorians pretended it didn't exist and our society acts as if it's the only thing that exists. God has a clear word for us. He's not anti-sex, He's pro-sex. God invented sex. Remember how it all started? Adam was alone, but God saw it wasn't good for him to be alone, so He made Eve. When Adam first saw Eve, he said, "Bone of my bone and flesh of my flesh." That's Hebrew for "Yes!" He was excited. I sometimes wonder what Adam really said to Eve. What was his line? Men are so insecure. The natural male response would be to have someone else call Eve to see if she liked him before he talked to her. But he couldn't do that. He couldn't say, "Haven't I seen you before?" That wouldn't work. He couldn't have someone set up a blind date. There wasn't anyone around. He couldn't do his Elvis impersonation. She wouldn't know Elvis. He probably just said, "I'm Adam."

God put them together, and He gave them a clear word about how to have long-term happiness and how to avoid pain. There were forbidden waters. The members of that first family had difficulty because they did what God had given the clear word not to do. They experienced great pain. They lost their family. God has given our society a very clear word about what to do. There are many of us who look at that word and dismiss it. Families are being destroyed. Our whole society is at risk.

God's clear word—the Seventh Commandment—is found in Exodus 20:14: "You shall not commit adultery." Remember that every commandment in the Old Testament, except that about the Sabbath day, has its counterpart in the New Testament. In Matthew 5:27-28 it says, "You have heard that it was said to those of old, 'You shall not commit adultery.' But I say to you that whoever looks at a woman to lust for her has already committed adultery with her in his heart." God is pro-sex, but He wants to give you something that will help you in this area of life. He wants you to have the very best. He doesn't want you to settle for second best. If you look at sex as just a union of two bodies and ignore the spiritual dimension, you're always going to settle for second best. Or in our society, maybe even third best, fourth best or fifth best. God gives us a very clear word about how to avoid pain and how to have real pleasure in our life.

The commandment about murder involves destroying another person, but often adultery destroys many people. It brings great pain. God is very strong and clear about this area. Adultery defies God. Monogamy and monotheism are very closely related in the Bible. God wants you to have one God, and He wants you to have one wife, one husband, one sexual relationship. Idolatry and adultery are interchanged in the Old Testament. We've known for years that you can only serve one master. God makes it clear that we are the ones who have the capacity to defy God in our sexual relationship. If passion controls you, passion becomes your god, and God is not your God. Adultery degrades people because you see them just for their bodies and not for their whole person. You look at the body instead of the soul, and engage in casual or recreational sex. Sex can mean death, because when you sleep with someone, you sleep with everybody else with whom they've slept.

If you're a teenager or unmarried, I would give you some advice. Use God's plan for your life. Wait. Use that positive protection of God's principles in your life. One girl was being pressured to give in by some other girls. She looked at them and said, "I can be like you anytime I want to be, but you can never be like me." Wait.

Adultery defies God, it degrades people, and it denies true love. We are all looking for love. There are four Greek words for love, and we'll look at two of them. Eros is erotic love. Affairs or adultery are usually based on erotic love. Erotic love asks, "What can you do for me? What can you do to give me pleasure?" That's not true love—that won't last. The urge to merge will dwindle. True love is agape love. That's God's love for us—it lasts forever. Agape love is not, "What can I get from you?" it's "What can I give to you?" That's true love.

People having an affair often say they're in love. They're usually just in lust, because they want something from someone else, and what they give to that other person they take from their mate. You will never experience true love unless you experience it God's way. Adultery denies true love and devastates families. The forbidden waters will give you a thrill, but in the long term they will only bring pain. Family members will be involved, and there will be great difficulty, even devastating consequences. God gave this commandment in the context of marriage. The foundation of society is that we want one woman with one man for life. Adultery is as much a trust issue as it is a sexual issue. If we can't trust, the foundation of society crumbles.

A little boy hammered a nail into the dining room table. He didn't realize how much damage there was until he already had hammered it in. His father caught him and scolded him sternly. He said, "I'm sorry, Daddy. I'll pull it out." As he pulled it out, tears filled his eyes and he said, "Daddy, the hole won't go away." Adultery puts a hole in the soul. There's a hurt there that's probably like no other hurt. That's why God is so strong. He doesn't want His people to experience that. He tells us to be careful in that area. It devastates families, and it destroys society. Remember the context of the Ten Commandments. God is telling the Jews that they are His chosen people. He has taken them out of slavery. He is sending them to the promised land. God knew if His chosen people started to fool around with sex that they would destroy the relationship; there would be no future.

It's the same today. A prominent historian said this, "After a study of 88 civilizations, I have come to the conclusion that human society is free to choose either to display great energy or to enjoy sexual freedom. The evidence is that they can't do both for more than one generation." It only takes one generation to decide that they are going to do what they want to do. They don't care who they hurt. It doesn't matter what society says. It doesn't matter what God says. They are going to do what they want to. A sociologist from Harvard says this: "Unless there's a change in America, we are doomed for the ash heap. No civilization, no empire, no nation has survived obsession with sex and impurity. This disease is eating the heart out of America."

Adultery destroys our society, and then, most crucial for us in the church today, it demeans Christianity. Remember David? David committed adultery, and the prophet told him he was forgiven of his sin. Nevertheless, he gave great occasion for the enemies of God to blaspheme. His sin was forgiven but the enemies of God talked about him and laughed, blasphemed. When Christian leaders fall, that's what happens. When Christian workers are involved in that kind of behavior, people look and laugh and say, "They don't really believe God. They don't really trust God for their happiness. They're doing what they want to."

Remember that God is pro-sex. He wants us to enjoy the best, but He knows that we need boundaries in our life. We have examples of necessary boundaries all around us. I love to have a fire in the fireplace. We can relax and enjoy it. The fire in the fireplace gives us great pleasure, but that same fire in my favorite chair would cause pain. God's word is to keep the fire in the fireplace. Contain it so you can enjoy it, so you'll have pleasure instead of pain. In the short run, the forbidden waters are exciting, but they will bring devastation in the long run.

1 Corinthians 6:18-20 says, "Flee sexual immorality. Every sin that a man does is outside the body, but he who commits sexual immorality sins against his own body. Or do you not know that your body is the temple of the Holy Spirit who is in you, whom you have from God, and you are not your own? For you were bought at a price; therefore glorify God in your body and in your spirit, which are God's." Every time I read that text, I think of the Old Testament story of Joseph. He was in Egypt, and his boss, Potiphar, was gone. Mrs. Potiphar—maybe her name was Patti, I don't know—Patti Potiphar came and said, "Joseph, I want to sleep with you. I want to have sex with you. It's all right. It will give you pleasure. It will give me pleasure." Remember what Joseph did? He ran. He literally ran out of the situation. Why? Because he knew that was not God's plan for his life. He knew that God had a better plan. He knew that God wanted to work through him to bless many people. He knew that one day God would have a woman for him and one day he would have a family and that God wanted him to prosper. He counted on the promise of God more than the passion of the moment. God did bless him, and he had an incredible, wonderful life. He left a great heritage. Why? He counted on the promise of God instead of the pleasure of the moment.

Either you'll be a promise keeper or you'll be a pleasure seeker. God keeps His promises. His ultimate promise was Jesus Christ, who came and gave us eternal life, although it cost Him His life, although He had to die on the cross. The promise was kept so that we may have eternal life. He has other promises for your life, and He wants to bless you. He wants you to have a great life in the long term. We will either accept that promise or we'll be a pleasure seeker. We won't have any authority in our life. We'll be the authority, or if we say we believe in God, we'll think God is just someone up there who will do what we want to make us happy. We'll do anything for pleasure. It doesn't matter whom it hurts. It doesn't matter whom it devastates. We give ourselves pleasure. Promise keepers are person centered — first centered in Christ and then centered in each other. But pleasure seekers are passion driven. They're controlled by their appetite, and it destroys whatever gets in their way. Ultimately, that leads to unhappiness and then death.

That's not what we hear out in the secular world. I know. Adultery is the main topic of most sitcoms. It's something to laugh about. You don't hear the Seventh Commandment on our current television programs or movies. You don't hear it on MTV. You don't hear it on public broadcasting. The psychologist and bestselling author, John Bradshaw, is often on public broadcasting. He's the guru of what I call pleasure-seeking spirituality. He never tires of telling us to listen to our wonder child within. Follow your intuitions. Let me read to you from his book, Homecoming. He said, "Once I worked with a woman who was, in spite of a seemingly stable marriage, insistent that she needed a divorce. Her husband was well off, loved her, and wanted to work out their problems. They had six children. My client spoke with a sense of urgency saying this, 'If I stay in this marriage, I know I'll never be what God created me to be. My life is on the line. I can't tell you why. I just feel it, and I know I am right." That's the New Age philosophy. If God's inside of you, you ought to do whatever you feel. If I did that, my life would be a wreck I wouldn't even be here today. Do you realize I've never felt like getting up in the morning? Never in my life have I felt like that. I have never felt like getting out of bed. If you live your life according to feelings, you're going to be in serious trouble. Bradshaw goes on to say, "She filed for divorce. The old order went bananas," he chuckled. "Her Baptist pastor was horrified, her Bible study group began a weekly prayer vigil, and her husband blamed me." I wonder why. Five years later she wrote him, and this is his testimonial. She said she was now listening to that wonder child and she now owns her own company. She was making a half a million dollars a year, and she had a wonderful friendship with a special man. Her wonder child had won out. But Bradshaw doesn't say if he had gotten letters from the six children. He doesn't say what their life was like. He doesn't say anything about the husband who was left. He doesn't say what their lives were like, because if you're passion driven, you don't care about other people. You just care about yourself, the wonder child. Have you ever been around a wonder child? Have you ever been around a three- or four-year-old for a long period of time? He's basically a snot-nosed brat. He does what he wants to do when he wants to do it. How would you like to have a society of wonder children? We may have it now. God says that's not the way to live. Morality is not doing what your wonder child wants. Morality is not doing what you desire. Morality is not doing what comes naturally. Morality is not even doing what's politically correct. Morality is doing what is spiritually correct. Morality is doing what God says and relying on His promises, not your passion.

What's the bottom line? If you're committed to not commit adultery, you have to work on your marriage. You have to decide that's where you're going to stay. If the grass is greener on the other side, you're always going to be tempted by it. So what do you do? You work on your own yard. Where is the grass greener? The grass is greener where you water it, where you take care of it. I've been married for over 25 years, and I think the grass is so green in my yard I don't even want to look at somebody else's yard.

When working on your marriage keep several things in mind. Women, remember that men are ten-year-old boys grown up. They want to be admired. Your husband wants you to talk about how wonderful he is. That's important to him. Men, just as you need approval and admiration, a woman needs security. Your wife wants to know she's number one. She comes before everything. She wants to know she has Blue Cross/Blue Shield. She wants to know that if she is ill or injured that the bills will be paid. That's security to her. A woman wants to be listened to. A man falls in love by what he sees, and a woman falls in love by what she hears.

I saw a couple at the mall. She was a good-looking lady, and she was married to a guy who was fat and ugly. I can't say that, can I? That's not politically correct. He wasn't fat, he was nutritionally enhanced. He wasn't ugly, he was aesthetically challenged. You get the picture? They're happy. How did he get her? Did she owe him money and couldn't pay? How did he do it? I'll tell you how he did it. He listened to her. Women want to talk, and they want you to listen, and they want you to respond. It's amazing what will happen. Remember women, men fall in love with what they see. Make sure the grass is greener at home. Look good. One guy said, "What's the difference between a wife and a girlfriend?" The other guy said, "About 30 pounds." Your husband wants you to look as good as you can, be as attractive as you can. Work at that relationship. Make it positive. Studies reveal that relationships that succeed have four elements: time, touching, talking, and trust. Work on the relationship God has given you.

You may have already blown it and already gone through one or more marriages. There are many of us that are beyond that and are into new relationships. Some are in a situation they shouldn't be in. They have already blown it. What can they do? Look at Romans 5:20-21: "Moreover the law entered that the offense might abound. But where sin abounded, grace abounded much more, so that as sin reigned in death, even so grace might reign through righteousness to eternal life through Jesus Christ our Lord." Thank goodness that God has more grace than we have sin, that His blood washes away all sin. As David, who committed adultery, says, "Though my sins be as scarlet they shall be as white as snow."

Adultery is not the unpardonable sin. The unpardonable sin is rejecting the person who has the ability to pardon, and that's Jesus Christ. If you don't know Him today, you are looking for love in all the wrong places. You will only find that love in Jesus Christ and only through Him can you properly love the people in your life. God wants you to commit that you are going to follow His principles, live His way that your joy may be full. To those people who have blown it, who have committed adultery, what is our response? Our response should be the same as God's response. We should never forget that we're a community of forgiven sinners. We don't condone the sin, but we don't condemn the sinner. Here's how Jesus responded to a woman called adulterer. She was caught in the act, and they brought her to Jesus. John 8:10-11 says, "When Jesus had raised Himself up and saw no one but the woman, He said to her, 'Woman, where are those accusers of yours? Has no one condemned you?' She said, No one, Lord.' And Jesus said to her, 'Neither do I condemn you; go and sin no more." If you've already blown it, Jesus would say to you that you are forgiven. Based on what He has done for you, you are forgiven, but He doesn't want you to have more pain. He wants you to go and sin no more. He wants you to develop another lifestyle. He wants you to start working on the relationship you have now. He wants you to make the grass as green as you can in your marriage. We will either be promise keepers or pleasure seekers. We can either be passion driven or people centered.

Young couples get hit with the three "D's": dishes, diapers, and debt. If you're not careful, you look at marriage as a burden.

Remember, Jesus said adultery starts in our mind. Perhaps in the beginning when you had problems in your marriage, you'd think, "I'm sorry. How can I be reconciled?" But later you may start thinking not "I'm sorry" but "It's her fault. It's his fault. She's the reason for my problems." God tells us to be careful. God wants you to stay in that relationship to grow to be what He created you to be. Don't forget the spiritual dimension of your marriage. I've probably seen it a hundred times. There's a couple that is happy and together and involved in church. Then, one or both stop loving the Lord and stop giving priority to the church. One or both start concentrating on loving themselves. Then one or both stop loving the other person. That is the demise of a marriage. God tells us to be careful. He wants you to enjoy what He's given you. He wants you to work at it.

Be a promise keeper and pass on the heritage that you have with your wife to the next generation. If you don't, America is in serious trouble. My mom and dad were married 53 years. Dad didn't leave me an inheritance, but he left me a heritage. It goes like this: there was a bus, and on the bus was a young man. The bus stopped, and an old man got on the bus and sat down by the young man. In his arms he cradled a dozen roses. It was Valentine's Day. The young man looked at the old man and said, "Boy, somebody sure is going to get a beautiful Valentine's present today." The old man looked at the flowers and said, "Yeah, they sure are beautiful." They chatted for a few minutes, and the old man said, "Do you have a girlfriend?" He said, "I sure do. Matter of fact, I've got this card." He picked up the card and said, "I'm giving this card to my girlfriend today." They went along in silence, and when they came to a stop, the old man got up to get off. Just as he started to get off, he took the dozen roses and he placed them on the lap of the young man. He said, "Look, my wife would want you to have these roses today, and I'll tell her that I gave them to you. See ya." He got off the bus before the kid could say thank you. He looked out the bus window and saw the man go through the gates of the cemetery. What the old man gave was a heritage that he lived. I hope that when I am an old man, I can pass that same heritage to some young man. God's principles work. God doesn't want you to have pain. God is a God of love and mercy. If we don't commit to be promise keepers and pass down that heritage, there's not much hope for our society.

Some of you are looking for love, and you've never found true love in Jesus Christ; therefore, you have a hard time loving other people. There are others of you who have a hole in your soul. There are some past sins for which you haven't asked forgiveness. You need to get it straight. You've been all gummed up. We have a God of mercy who wants to clean you out. He wants you to experience the joy that He has for you.

No Shortcuts

The next commandment talks about stealing. I heard a story of a man in ancient times who was to be executed because he had stolen some food. Before he was executed, he told the king, "I have a secret. I know how to plant a seed one day and an apple tree will come up the next day. I don't want to die because the secret will die with me. I would like to pass it on." The next day they went out and dug a hole. The man said, "The seed has to be planted in this hole, and it has to be planted by someone who has never stolen anything. Now, me, I'm a thief, so I can't plant the seed. Whoever plants the seed can never have stolen anything or it won't work. Find someone who has never taken anything." The king knew he had stolen so he didn't want to be the one, because he knew the tree wouldn't grow. He checked all around the cabinet, all of his officials. He couldn't find anyone who was willing to plant the seed, because everyone had taken something. The man said, "Here all your people in power have taken things and I have stolen a little food to live. Why should you execute me?" Of course the king realized that he shouldn't execute the man, and the man went free.

We all have a little thief in us, and when we take shortcuts, we find out they have unbelievable consequences. I heard about a man who saw an expensive motor home. He needed some gas, so he thought he'd siphon it out. He crawled underneath and put his rubber tube into the tank and started to suck to get the gasoline flowing. All of a sudden, the owner of the motor home heard an incredible noise, ran outside, and turned on the lights. There he saw the man gagging, writhing on the ground. The thief had put the rubber tube in the sewer tank, not the gasoline tank. The owner decided not to press charges. He thought the man had been punished enough.

What does God have to say to us about stealing? Exodus 20:15 says, "You shall not steal." Proverbs 20:23 puts it this way, "Diverse weights are an abomination to the Lord, and dishonest scales are not good." Remember the context of the Ten Commandments. The Israelites were leaving slavery and going to a land of opportunity. These people had never had the opportunity to acquire wealth or to own anything. Now they could. God says that because they had this opportunity, He wanted them to understand that they don't steal from other people. In this commandment, God is saying that ownership is important, and He puts great value on private property. In Exodus 22, God goes into great detail about what happens if you're caught stealing. For example, if you steal one man's ox, you have to give him five oxen back. You steal one sheep, you have to give four sheep back. That's restitution—if you take something from someone else, you have to restore more than what you stole in the first place. Our society would be better off if we understood that restitution is important. People who steal should be made to give back more than they took.

God has given us marvelous opportunities, but He tells us not to steal from other people. There are many ways to steal. Proverbs 20 says that stealing can involve deception. We deceive—use dishonest scales—in order to get more. We charge more than things are worth. That's unethical behavior. A young man asked his dad, "What is ethics?" He said, "Your Uncle Billy and I are in business together. Suppose a customer comes in and buys something worth $10 but mistakenly gives me a $20 bill for it. Now ethics would be if I split that extra $10 with your Uncle Billy." That's not exactly it, folks. God doesn't want you to deceive people. We can deceive people in any number of ways. A little boy came home with two ice cream cones and said, "Mama, I got these ice cream cones free." She said, "Well, Son, I hope you didn't swipe them." "You know I wouldn't do that," he said. "I said to the lady behind the counter, 'I want a vanilla and a chocolate.' And I got the vanilla in one hand and the chocolate in the other hand. I said, 'Just get the money out of my pocket right there, except don't bother my pet snake." That's using deceit to get something that you're really not entitled to. Good business would be to say, "Honesty is the best policy"; but God says that honesty is the only policy. Be honest in your relationships and make sure you're not involved in white collar crime, insider trading, or false advertising.

One way to steal is to slander or gossip. Someone said, "Who steals my wallet steals cash, but he who steals my good name robs me." We can degrade a person's name, destroy his or her reputation, or deny a person the benefit of the doubt. We steal when we leave a financial deficit to the next generation. We spend not only what we have but also what we don't have, and the next generation is saddled with a deficit they have to deal with. I read an article about social security that said unless things change, social security will run out of money the year I am 66. I was really thrilled to hear that. I'm going to have to work forever. When we take what isn't ours, we take from someone else.

Some college professors steal the faith of college students. They think they're smarter than God. They say that if God really does exist, He is real sick and surely couldn't give you eternal life. There was a philosophy professor—an unbeliever—who wanted to console his mother, who was on her deathbed. He said, "Mother, hold on. Mother, you've got to hold on." She looked up at him and said, "Son, I can't hold on. I don't have anything to hold on to. You have robbed me of my faith."

Deuteronomy 24:14-15 says: "You shall not oppress a hired servant who is poor and needy, whether one of your brethren or one of the aliens who is in your land within your gates. Each day you shall give him his wages, and not let the sun go down on it, for he is poor and has set his heart on it; lest he cry out against you to the Lord, and it be sin to you." What's God saying there? Don't take advantage of people who work for you. Don't pay them less than what they're worth and pay them on time. Employees can also steal from the employer. You're guilty of fraud if you don't give an honest day's work for what you are paid. If you're lazy on the job or take time off when you're supposed to be working, you steal from your employer. God knows our tendency is to use people because we love money. He wants you to love people and use money.

The question is not, "How little can I do and still get as much as I can?" It's, "How much can I do?" The positive of this commandment is that there is a way, without shortcuts, to obtain things in this world, to meet some of your desires. It's not your way, it's God's way. 2 Thessalonians 3:10 says, "For even when we were with you, we commanded you this: If anyone will not work, neither shall he eat." Ephesians 4:28 puts it this way, "Let him who stole steal no longer, but rather let him labor, working with his hands what is good, that he may have something to give him who has need." Work so you can give. Psalm 90:17, probably written by Moses, says this, "And let the beauty of the Lord our God be upon us, and establish the work of our hands for us; Yes, establish the work of our hands."

Moses says that work is important. Work is what people ought to do. Work gives dignity to life. Work gives you a reason to get up in the morning. The Bible says, "The work of your hands," because that's the kind of work there was in that day and age. In our time, whether you use your brain at Sandia Labs or Intel or whatever you do, do it, the Bible says, to the glory of God. It's important that we work, that we do the very best we can do. If you look at the great men of the Bible, they were all hard workers. Think of Noah. God showed up and said, "Noah, I want you to build an ark, and I want you to build it in two weeks because rain is going to come." Noah said, "Two weeks. There's no way I can build that ark in two weeks." God said, "Noah, how long can you tread water?" And Noah said, "Two weeks. I think I can do it God. I think I can do it."

God is saying that there's no difference between secular work and Christian work. There's no difference whether you work at the church or whether you work in the business world. God says that everything you do, you do to the glory of God. Christ should make a difference in your work habits. There was a young maid who worked in a wealthy home. She became a Christian. She applied for membership in the church where Spurgeon, a famous preacher, was the pastor. The committee was probing for some evidence of her conversion. Spurgeon asked her, "Is there any evidence which indicates a change of heart?" She replied, "Now I don't sweep the dirt under the rugs in the house where I'm employed." Spurgeon turned to the men and said, "It is enough. We will receive her." Her new faith had made a difference in how she lived her daily life. God wants people to work. If this country destroys the incentive for people to work, we're in trouble. People who can't work should be taken care of, but everyone should work. It's for their good. It's for their dignity.

There's a modern-day parable about a little red hen. It goes like this: Once upon a time there was a little red hen who scratched about the barnyard. She uncovered some grains of wheat. She called her neighbors and said, "If we plant this wheat, we shall have bread to eat. Who will help me plant it?" "Not I," said the cow. "Not I," said the duck. "Not I," said the pig. "Not I," said the goose. "I will then," said the little red hen and she did. The wheat grew tall and ripened into golden grain. "Who will help me reap my wheat?" asked the little red hen. "Not I," said the duck. "Out of my classification," said the pig. "I'll lose my seniority," said the cow. "I'll lose my unemployment compensation," said the goose. "Then I will," said the little red hen and she did. At last it came time to bake the bread. "Who will help me bake the bread?" asked the little red hen. "That would be overtime for me," said the cow. "I'd lose my welfare benefits," said the duck. "If I'm going to be the only helper, that's discrimination," said the goose. "Then I will," said the little red hen and she baked the five loaves and held them up for all the neighbors to see. They all wanted some. In fact, they demanded a share, but the little red hen said, "No. I can eat the five loaves all by myself." "Excess profits," cried the cow. "Capitalistic leech," cried the duck "I demand equal rights," shouted the goose. The pig just grunted. They hurriedly painted picket signs and marched around the barnyard shouting obscenities. The government agent came and said to the little red hen, "You must not be greedy." "But I earned the bread," said the little red hen. "Exactly," said the agent. "That's the wonderful free-enterprise system. Anyone in the barnyard can earn as much as he wants, but under government regulations, the productive worker must divide his product with the idle." They lived happily ever after, but the little red hen's neighbors wondered why she never again baked bread. We have to be careful in this country that we don't destroy the incentive to work because God says, "Work is honorable."

God doesn't want you to steal from others. He doesn't want you to steal from your business. He doesn't want you to steal from the government. He wants you to be up front and above board in all your communications. He doesn't want you to steal by deception. He doesn't want you to take any shortcuts. Then finally, God says that He doesn't want you to steal from Him, either. Psalm

24:1 says, "The earth is the Lord's, and all its fullness, the world and those who dwell therein." God has created everything. God's made me. God's made you. Malachi 3:8, 10 says, "Will a man rob God? Yet you have robbed Me! But you say, 'In what way have we robbed You?' In tithes and offerings. Bring all the tithes into the storehouse, that there may be food in My house, and try Me now in this,' says the Lord of hosts, 'If I will not open for you the windows of heaven and pour out for you such blessing that there will not be room enough to receive it."

This is a philosophy of life. What we have here is the theology of material things. God says that all things come from Him, and because He loves you so much, He gives you these things with a loving heart. He wants you to enjoy these things. He wants you to have a nice home. He wants you to work hard and drive a good car that doesn't break down. God also knew there was a dark side to wealth. Remember the Ten Commandments? The Israelites were going into the promised land, and God knew that they would have the ability to accumulate wealth. If you're not careful, wealth can take on the same characteristics as deity. You can let your security be in what you have instead of Who you have. You can count on your money for your security, and your money can become your god.

In the Old Testament the tithe to be given to the Lord was a tenth. It was the amount set aside that they were not to touch because it was God's. God has always worked that way. Remember the Garden of Eden? God told Adam and Eve they had this wonderful garden. They didn't plant any of these trees. It's a gift from God. He gave them all of this, but there's one tree He didn't want them to partake of. There's one thing that they were not to steal from, to take away from, because He wanted them to be reminded daily that this stuff isn't God, that He is God, and that He gave it all to them. When the Israelites went on to the Promised Land, there was a wealthy city called Jericho with an abundance of silver, gold, all kinds of loot. God told them to leave it all. He was going to give them the victory. They would conquer the city, but they were not to take any of the silver or gold. Why? He wanted it to be an offering to Him.

He wanted them to acknowledge that He is God. There were something they should not touch, and that silver and gold are not God. He is the one they would trust. God also said that there should be part of their income, part of their material things set aside to God. When you don't do this, you're not really robbing God—God has all He wants. You're robbing yourself, because once you take God off the throne and make material things your god, you have a very miserable existence. The fact is God wants to bless you. God wants to give you resources, but so many of you won't give Him a chance. That's what Malachi says. God wants to show you how much He can bless you, to show you how much peace, love, and joy He can give you if you'll just give Him a chance.

I've been with wealthy parents who say they have great resources they'd love to give their children but can't. The lifestyle of the kids is such that they would take all of this money and use it up on drugs and alcohol and gambling. They would take these resources and make themselves more miserable. It would be worse for them to have it than not to have it. They would love to be able to give it to them. That's the way God looks at some of us. We are literally robbing ourselves of God's blessings because of our lifestyle, because we refuse to acknowledge who God is. He wants to bless you. Just try Him, and He'll pour out the blessings like you've never seen before.

Arthur Berry was a jewel thief during the Roaring '20s. He was a distinguished man who only stole from the very best people. Legend had it that you had to be in the social register before Arthur Berry would even break into your house. It became a prestigious thing to be broken into by Arthur Berry, because people knew that you had good stuff. He did that for many years and built a great reputation, but one time he didn't make it. He was shot three times through glass. He was bleeding, glass all in him, when the police arrived. Arthur Berry looked up at those police and he made a decision. He said, "I'm not going to do this anymore." It's easy to make those decisions with bullets and glass in you. They took him to jail and he served 18 years. When they let him out he went to New England and lived a quiet life. He was such a model citizen that they gave him an award. Because of that award it became known that he was Arthur Berry, the jewel thief. Reporters came from all over the country to interview him. One young man asked him, "Mr. Berry, you stole from some of the wealthiest people who have ever lived. Let me ask you, who is the person you stole the most from?" Arthur Berry said without hesitation, "Young man, I can tell you that for sure. I stole the most from myself. You see, if I had taken all of that ability and hadn't tried to take a shortcut, I could have been a successful businessman on Wall Street. Two-thirds of my adult life was spent in prison. I missed out on being with my family. The man I stole from the most was myself." God says to not steal from yourself. Don't take any shortcuts. Do it My way so I can give you all the blessings that I have.

Breaking Free

The Ninth Commandment has to do with telling the truth. There was a commercial for Isuzu cars and trucks. A reptilian kind of guy on the television says, "Isuzu trucks only cost $9. They get 94 miles to the gallon, and if you buy one soon, you'll get a free house." Underneath, in white block letters, are the words, "He's lying." But he keeps on talking. He says, "They go 300 miles per hour. They seat the same number of people as the Astrodome, and they're roomy enough to carry the state of Texas." The words appear again: "He's lying." Isuzu sales went up 21 percent the first year that ad aired. The ad agency said that young people today are cynical. They've been lied to before, and they're amused by the shocking, simple truth of the liar commercials. That's the kind of society in which we live. We know people are lying and yet we buy from them anyway.

There's a growing sense of concern in this country that we've become a generation of liars. Society has gone too far. In an address to Duke University, Ted Koppel of ABC's Nightline said, "We've actually convinced ourselves that slogans will save us. Shoot up if you must, but use clean needles. Enjoy sex whenever and with whomever you wish, but use a condom." Then Koppel added this sharp rebuke, "The answer is no. Not because it isn't cool or smart or because you might end up in jail or dying in an AIDS ward, but because it's wrong, because we've spent 5,000 years as a race of rational human beings trying to drag ourselves out of the primeval slime by searching for truth and moral absolutes. In its purest form, truth is not a polite tap on the shoulder, it's a howling reproach. What Moses brought down from Mount Sinai were not the Ten Suggestions."

Telling the truth can be very difficult, because when you tell someone the truth, they look at your life. I heard about a music director who had someone in the choir who just could not sing. He tried to get the guy out of the choir. He couldn't. Finally he went to the pastor and said, "Pastor, you've got to get this guy out of the choir. He's messing up everything. He cannot sing." The pastor met with the guy, and he tried to give him some hints. It was evident the guy wasn't going to leave the choir. Finally the pastor said, "I'm going to tell you the undiluted truth. There are six people in the choir who say you have an awful voice and that you cannot sing." And he said, "Well, Pastor, that's nothing. There are 50 people in the congregation who tell me you can't preach." When you tell the truth, people are going to start looking at your life. Maybe that's one of the reasons why we don't tell the truth.

There's a book called *A Day America Told the Truth* that came out in 1991. The research shows that 91 percent of Americans lie routinely; 36 percent confessed to dark, important lies; 86 percent regularly lied to their parents; and 75 percent lie to friends. We all lie at some time. A pastor saw a group of kids standing around a stray dog, talking. He said, "What are you doing?" They said, "We're all telling lies, and the kid who can tell the biggest lie is going to get this dog." The pastor was just horrified and said, "I can't believe you're doing that. At your age, I never told a lie." The kids looked at each other, shrugged, and said, "Well, I guess you get the dog." We all lie. Let me share some modem lies that you'll pick up on pretty clearly. "The check is in the mail." "I'll start my diet tomorrow." "One size fits all." This is from my dentist, "This is going to hurt a little." "Your luggage isn't lost, it's only misplaced." "I only need ten minutes of your time." And then maybe the biggest lie is, "I'm from the government, and I'm here to help you."

The Ninth Commandment is found in Exodus 20:16, "You shall not bear false witness against your neighbor." Initially the prohibition was against bearing false witness in court. In that day, if people were taken to court, they'd pay someone to lie for them so they didn't have to bear the consequences of what they had done. The Old Testament book of Deuteronomy goes into great detail about what to do to someone who lies. It says when you go to court; make sure you tell the truth. Don't cover for anyone else. The New Testament, especially in Galatians, takes the commandment even further. It talks about slander and gossip and other ways of being a false witness. Ephesians 4:15 says, "but, speaking the truth in love, we may grow up in all things into Him who is the head—Christ." Verse 25 says, "Therefore, putting away lying..." Remember in all these commandments, when you stop doing something, you have to start doing something else. "...putting away lying, 'Let each one of you speak truth with his neighbor' for we are members of one another." In other words, we are all in this together. God wants you to speak the truth. Not only that, He wants you to live the truth. He wants you to do what you say you're going to do. The greatest sign of immaturity is to say one thing and then not to do it because something better comes along. "I was going to do my homework, but then the movie came on." "I was going to go to work, but then I was just so sleepy." You end up not being successful in the world because of your immaturity. God says to speak the truth, to live the truth.

Telling the truth also means that you understand, as it says in Ephesians, that you speak the truth in love. Sometimes telling someone the truth can wound them and hurt them. God wants us to be gentle with those people. Proverbs lists seven things that God hates. Two of those things have to do with dishonesty of the tongue. God says, "I hate dishonesty. I hate lying because my character is a character of truth." The Bible says God can never lie and because of that, He can't stand people who lie.

How are we false witnesses? We slander, gossip, and distort the truth. Sometimes we do that to escape punishment. If you've done something wrong, what's the first thing you do? You lie. Four guys were late for school, and the teacher asks, "What happened?" They had their story together. "We had a flat tire." It worked well until she sat them down and said, "OK, everyone get out a piece of paper and each one of you write down which tire was flat." They had a story but they didn't have all of the story. They got into trouble. Why? They were lying to escape punishment. Some people lie for revenge, thinking they can put other people down and build themselves up. Some people gossip, taking what people tell them and embellish. They have all of the details but none of the facts. As one lady said, "I better stop what I'm telling you. I've already told you more than they told me." We tear people down, hurt people, wound people. Don't put people down, bring people up. Tell God about the situation. Don't tell everyone. The Third Commandment says not to take God's name in vain." The Ninth Commandment says not to take your neighbor's name in vain.

Silence can be a way of bearing false witness. Do you realize that sometimes by not saying something, you're lying? When someone is saying something untrue about another, and you just sit there and don't come to their defense, then you don't stand for what's right and true. There are many other ways to bear false witness. One way is to give the impression that we're better than everyone else, that we have it all together, that we have all the answers. We have the idea that we're so spiritual, that everyone else is beneath us. The fact is we have a problem of lying in this country. Our politicians have a problem. We make jokes about it. "How do you know when a politician is lying? When his lips are moving."

Where did it all begin? Why did we become liars? Why is our nature bent toward telling an untruth? Psalm 51:5, 6 says, "Behold, I was brought forth in iniquity, and in sin my mother conceived me. Behold, You desire truth in the inward parts, and in the hidden part You will make me to know wisdom." John 8:44 gets more specific, "You are of your father the devil, and the desires of your father you want to do. He was a murderer from the beginning, and does not stand in the truth, because there is no truth in him. When he speaks a lie, he speaks from his own resources, for he is a liar and the father of it." You know why we have a bent toward lying? It's because of our ancestry. We go back to Adam and Eve, and Eve was convinced by Satan, the original liar, that God was not true. Satan convinced Eve that the tree was OK. "God lied to you. God's not telling you all of the truth." Satan, who is the liar, made God out to be a liar. Satan, who is the father of lies, convinced Eve. Lying is Satan's native language. When you lie, you speak the language of Satan himself. Satan is never more proud than when you lie because he knows that you are in difficulty. His job is to destroy you, murder you, and keep you from being what God created you to be. The way he does that is to lie to you. He tells you to repeat those lies to other people. That is his master plan.

The Bible says God is the opposite. In Titus it says that God can never lie, that God wants to build you up, and that God wants you to have a good life. Lying leads to destruction. Lying leads to death. The first great persecution of the church came from a lie. Nero, drunken Nero, fiddled while Rome burned. He was actually the cause of the fire, but he blamed it on the Christians, and all those Christians were persecuted. Why? Because of a lie. The greatest atrocity of modern times was that Hitler had six million

Jews killed. Why? Because he perpetrated a lie that they were an inferior race and had to be exterminated. Because of that lie, there was destruction. Jesus was crucified because of a lie. False witnesses accused him.

Lying leads to destruction even in our modern times. A guy wrote this to Ann Landers: "I was a complete liar who started young. Although my parents did all they could to stop it, I kept lying. My problem was trying to impress people. My life never seemed glamorous enough. Here's a short history of what happens to a liar. I went to school and lied to my friends, trying to look like a big shot. When I got out of high school, I had no friends, so I started to look for new ones. By then, lying became a way of life. In order to support the lies, I needed more money. So I wrote checks I couldn't cover. I also impersonated a naval officer and later a successful businessman. My wife found out that I had totally misrepresented myself and admitted to friends and businesses I never had. She left me. The same thing happened with my second wife. I decided I had to change. Shortly after I married my third wife, I went to prison for passing bad checks. She divorced me while I was in prison. This advice is for the kid who lies. Please think about the future. A lie not only hurts you but it poisons all of your relationships. I'll get out of prison someday and when I do I vow to tell the truth. I'll probably still be called a liar, but after a while, people will find out they can trust me. I'm 26 years old, and by the time I'm 50, I will have built a good reputation. A kind teacher once told me, 'A person's word is worth more than gold.' It's too bad it took me so long to wake up to that fact." Then he closes by saying, "If you're a liar, stop while you still have friends. I hope my letter will help someone who is where I was 15 years ago." Lying leads to destruction. Lying destroys relationships.

What do we do? 2 Timothy 2:24-26 says, "And a servant of the Lord must not quarrel but be gentle to all, able to teach, patient, in humility correcting those who are in opposition, if God perhaps will grant them repentance, so that they may know the truth, and that they may come to their senses and escape the snare of the devil, having been taken captive by him to do his will." Remember when you're lying, you're under Satan's spell. You're lying on his behalf. 1 John 5:19 says, "We know that we are of God, and the whole world lies under the sway of the wicked one. And we know that the Son of God has come and has given us an understanding, that we may know Him who is true; and we are in Him who is true, in His Son Jesus Christ. This is the true God and eternal life."

Our goal is to speak the truth, and the Bible says you can't speak the truth until you know the truth, until you know Jesus Christ. He's the one Who loves you and He's the one Who came to die for you to prove that love, and He's the one Who has the very best life possible for you. When you understand that, you understand that truth is good for you. Truth makes you what He wants you to be. Otherwise, you'll be in slavery. Remember the Ten Commandments were for God's people whom He brought out of slavery. God wanted them to have freedom, but He knew if they started to bear false witness, if they tried to give the impression that they were better than they really were, if they were not honest, they would end up in slavery again. They would be destroyed. So God gives them this commandment.

How are we to teach people? It says we are to teach them gently. We're to be patient, and we're to help them come to their senses. That's what we do every weekend. We teach people to come to their senses. Quit believing the lie. Believe the truth. Come to your senses, and do what God would have you do. Don't let Satan destroy you. You may be familiar with the books, *Born Free, Living Free,* and *Forever Free.* They were written by Joy Adamson, who raised lions in East Africa. She was known for her way with lions. Some years later, at age 69, she was attacked and killed by a lion. You see, she had grown careless and comfortable, believing that these were not lions, but that these were nice pets, and they would not hurt her. She believed a lie; a lie destroyed her. That's what Satan does. The Bible says Satan is like a lion. He wants to destroy you. His motive is murder and his method is lies. He wants to murder your marriage, your relationships, and your friendships. He wants to murder those dreams that God has put in your life. Satan does not want you to be what God wants you to be.

How do we handle this? In John 1:17 it says, "For the law was given through Moses, but grace and truth came through Jesus Christ." John 8:32 puts it this way, "And you shall know the truth, and the truth shall make you free." Freedom is linked to truth. Jesus told a story about a young man who told his father he was tired of being in slavery. He was tired of doing what his father told him to do. He wanted to leave. His father gave him his inheritance. The Bible says he went off to a far land and did exactly what he wanted to do. He discovered a strange truth—the more he did what he liked, the more he disliked what he did. The more he did things that gave him kicks, the more those things kicked back. He was a very miserable person who was in slavery to his own habits and his own sin. The Bible says he came to his senses and went back home to be with his father. That's what God's telling us to do. Come to your senses. Come back to God. You're in slavery to this world, and it is destroying you. We are bent by nature toward falsehood and the result is slavery and death. But God has the truth, and not only is it truth, it comes with grace. Here's a way to remember GRACE—God's Riches At Christ's Expense. That means that through Christ, once you believe in Him, you have all of the goodness of God. We are sinners—born to that nature—but Christ took our sin. Therefore, there's now no condemnation for those of us who are in Christ Jesus, and we have the goodness of God. God becomes our perfect father, our heavenly father. That's the gospel truth.

We always need to tell the truth. There's a lie out there that everyone's OK. God is going to accept everyone into Heaven. I read about a church in northern California that has portraits of famous people hanging in the vestibule. There are portraits of Socrates, Eleanor Roosevelt, Abraham Lincoln, Ghandi, and Jesus Christ. Written in beautiful gold letters under these portraits are the words, "And we are all children of God." I'm sure people walk by there every day and say how marvelous it is, the Universal Brotherhood of man, the Universal Fatherhood of God. We are all children of God. It's a benevolent statement. It's an inclusive statement, but it's a lie. We're not all children of God. It's a quote right out of the Bible, but it's only half the quote. Galatians says we are all children of God, but the rest of the verse says, "Through faith in our Lord Jesus Christ." That's how you become a child of God, only through faith in Jesus Christ. But Satan would want you to believe that's too narrow. I mean, this is the 21st century. It's not even politically correct. There can't be just one way. There has to be many different ways. You're not so bad. You're neighbor is just as bad you as you are. Look, he isn't worried. Satan infiltrates our world with lies. God tells the truth, He cannot lie. The truth is that Jesus is the way into God's heaven.

What's the bottom line? First of all, be very careful about what you say. Be very honest in your dealings with people. Don't put people down, lift people up. Let me give you a word that will help you. Before you say something about someone, I want you to first think THINK. A.W. Tozier came up with this thought many years ago. THINK stands for these words. "T" stands for True. Is what I'm going to say about this person True? Next, "H." Is it Helpful? "I." Is it Inspiring? Will it uplift the situation? Then "N." Is it Necessary? "K." Is it Kind? If you think about these words before you speak, it will help you not to bear false witness against your neighbor.

A pastor had a lady come to him. The lady said she had

said some awful things about him and she found out now they weren't true. She wanted to repent and get his pardon. He said, "What I'd like you to do is take this pillow that's filled with feathers, and I want you to go to the top of Nob Hill, the highest point in the city. I want you to take this pillowcase and let all the feathers fall all over the city." She went to Nob Hill and let out all the feathers. The wind took them—they blew right out. She came back with the pillowcase and said, "I've done what you asked me, now do I have your pardon?" He said, "No, not yet. Now I want you to go back and pick up all the feathers in the city, and then you'll have my pardon." He was saying that once those words are out, you cannot bring them back. Once that lie is told, it will do its worst. We are to be very careful about the things we say. Dishonesty will destroy relationships. Honesty is what relationships have to be built on. God says to stay right with Him. Stay right with others. Refuse to lie. When you lie, you're speaking the language of the devil. God says that you will have a good life if you don't lie.

We need to understand that we should not bear false witness. We are to tell the gospel truth. When I was growing up after the war, way back when, polio was a disease that crippled and killed. Jonas Salk discovered a vaccine which was mass produced. At our school we lined up and they gave us a pink solution in a sugar cube. I remember taking that pink sugar cube and putting it in my mouth. There is something called sin and we all have it. It cripples. You can lie about it, but ultimately it means death and destruction. There is a vaccine, and it's Jesus Christ, who cleanses you from all sin and who presents you perfect to God the Father. That's the Gospel truth. During those days I could have said, "I don't like pink stuff. I don't like the way this vaccine has been presented. I like chocolate. Unless you give me chocolate I'm not going to take it." Guess what? I could have been crippled and maybe even died from polio.

Why was this? There was only one vaccine and one cure. This is the gospel truth. There's only one vaccine and one cure for sin and that's Jesus Christ. If you've never accepted Him, today should be the day. Some of you have already done that, but your life has become a pattern of lies. Some of you teenagers are not honest with your parents. You tell lies, either to avoid punishment or to give the impression that you're doing what you're supposed to be doing. God says that your lies will cripple you. Your lies will destroy you. Lies are what Satan is using to murder you, and you need to give up that pattern of life. Others of us need to quit giving false impressions. We need to be honest in our relationships and to understand that the only way to be free is through Jesus Christ. Know the truth and let the truth set you free.

From Deed to Desire

The law as given in the Ten Commandments is negative because it can't make you love me, but, on a positive note, it can keep you from killing me or stealing from me. The law is for our protection. People say you can't legislate morality; and in a sense they're right. We don't try to legislate morality; we try to legislate against immorality. We try to keep people from killing other people.

The law protects us. I read about Gloria Aguilar of Moses Lake, Washington. She was pulled over by Deputy Jerry Anderson. He gave her three $66 traffic tickets. The offense was that two adults in the car were not wearing their seat belts, and Gloria's toddler was not buckled in the seat belt, either. Two days later, without warning, another car cut in front of Gloria's car, forcing her to broadside the other vehicle, but thanks to the incentive of the three traffic tickets, Gloria and her daughter were able to walk away from the totaled car because she had buckled up. "When I recognized Deputy Anderson at the County Fair later," Gloria says, "I went over to him and thanked him for giving me the three tickets, and I had to admit to him that if he had only given us a verbal warning, my daughter and I probably wouldn't be alive today." The law is for our protection.

By nature, the commandments tend to be negative. Jesus then fulfills the Ten Commandments and makes them positive. In this chapter we are at the last commandment, which is the hinge that goes from deed to desire. It leads us into the New Testament. The Tenth Commandment is about coveting. To covet means to have an inordinate desire for something. In a way, covet is an amoral word because Paul says we are to covet good gifts, good things. It's when we covet things that aren't ours, when we covet a little too much, that we have trouble. It goes back to the Adam Family, Adam and Eve. Remember what Eve did? Her problem wasn't that she looked at the forbidden fruit, it was that she listened to Satan. Satan said to Eve that God had not provided enough for her. If she just counted on God, she was not going to have any fun and she was not ever going to have enough resources. She had to go out and do something herself. She had to get that forbidden fruit. She not only looked at the fruit, but she listened to the voice of Satan. When we covet, we do and say dumb things. Yogi Berra once admitted how jealous he was of Mickey Mantle because Mickey Mantle could bat right-handed and left-handed. In that jealousy, Yogi said, "I'd give my right arm to be ambidextrous like him." Count on Yogi for a little stupidity. The fact is we all covet forbidden fruit. There's something about coveting the forbidden that creates a thrill and excitement.

I read about a man in California who was in court. He was being sentenced because he had killed a California condor, an endangered species. The judge had sentenced him and banged the gavel. As he did that the man asked if he could make a statement. The judge agreed. He wanted to tell the judge it was just unbeliev-able circumstances that caused him to kill that bird. He was lost in the woods for days, maybe even weeks. He was out of food, out of water, and he just fell down. He was literally unconscious. He knew he was going to die. He looked up at a tree, and there was that bird. It was making some noise and really he was trying to get it out of the way so he could die in peace. He threw a rock up there. Lo and behold, it hit the bird in the head and killed it. It fell down right before him. In his almost unconscious state, being so hungry; he just built a fire and ate it. That allowed him to survive. He was really sorry he did it, but there were extenuating circumstances. The judge said he had never heard a story quite like that. He was right; those were extenuating circumstances. He didn't see how he could sentence the man for anything. Anyone would have done the same thing under those circumstances. The man was free to go. The man started to get up, and the judge asked him a question, "What does a California condor taste like?" And the man without thinking said, "It's kind of a cross between a bald eagle and a spotted owl." There's something in us that likes to do things that are forbidden; we covet things that are not ours.

The Tenth Commandment is found in Exodus 20:17: "You shall not covet your neighbor's house; you shall not covet your neighbor's wife, nor his male servant, nor his female servant, nor his ox, nor his donkey, nor anything that is your neighbor's." Remember that Jesus says that everyone is our neighbor. Hebrews 13:5-6 puts it this way, "Let your conduct be without covetousness; be content with such things as you have. For He Himself has said, 'I will never leave you nor forsake you.' So we may boldly say: 'The Lord is my helper; I will not fear. What can man do to me?" Psalm 119:36, "Incline my heart to Your testimonies" — in other words, listen to God — "and not to covetousness. Turn away my eyes from looking at worthless things, and revive me in Your way."

Two signs that you're in danger of breaking this command-ment are excessive work and excessive debt. Tolstoy told a story about a peasant who was offered all the land that he could walk in one day. The peasant was so excited that he could get all this land that he took off walking early in the morning and walked all day long. Just as he got to the end of walking, he dropped dead. The desire to have more than he really needed is what cost him his life. Let me give you an updated illustration out of everyday life. I was in the yard working the other day, and I saw a bird scratching in the ground. The bird dug up a worm, flew to the garage, and dropped the worm in a bucket. Then it flew back over to where that dirt was and scratched around a little bit, found another worm, flew to the garage, and dropped that worm in the bucket. As I watched, the bird went bucket, dirt, worm, bucket, dirt, worm, and bucket. Before I knew it, the bird had filled up the bucket with worms. Worms were just pouring out of that bucket. Then the bird flew over and picked up the bucket with its beak and flew off. It made it about 100 feet in the air and died of a heart attack.

You don't believe me. The reason you don't believe me is because you know a bird is smarter than that. A bird isn't going to try to put worms in a bucket and carry that bucket. He takes it one worm at a time and one day at a time. That's how we guard against breaking this commandment. As soon as you catch up with your neighbors, they refinance again. One guy said, "How can I stay out of debt when my neighbors keep buying things I can't afford?" That's hard. Don't be caught in excessive debt. One family was bragging that their furniture went back all the way to Louis XIV. The wife said, "That's nothing. If we don't make this payment, our furniture goes back to Sears on the 15th." Guard against excessive debt. Guard against that passion to possess and the preoccupation with things.

Let me introduce you to Mr. and Mrs. Thing. They are a pleasant and successful couple, at least that's the evaluation of most people who tend to measure everything with a thing-o-meter. When the thing-o-meter is put to work in the life of Mr. and Mrs. Thing, the results are startling. There he is sitting down at a very expensive, luxurious thing, almost hidden by a large number of other things—things to sit on, things to look at, things to cook on, and things to eat from— all shiny and new. Things to clean with, things to wash with, things to clean, and things to wash, things to amuse, and things for pleasure, and things to watch, and things to play, things for the long hot summer, and things for the short cool winter, things for the big thing in which they live, and things for the garden, and things for the lounge, and things for the kitchen, and things for the bedroom, and things for four wheels, and things on two wheels, things to put on top of the four wheels, things to put behind the four wheels, and things to add to the interior of the thing on four wheels. Things, things, things, and there in the middle are Mr. and Mrs. Thing, pleased with their things. Thinking of more things to add to their things, secure in their castle of things. Well, Mr. Thing, I have some bad news for you.

I just want you to know that your things can't last. They will pass. Maybe you'll take them to the secondhand thing dealer, or maybe tote them off to the thing yard. What about all those things in your house? When it's time to go to bed and put out the dog, make sure you lock the door and hope some thief doesn't come in and take all your things. That's the way life goes, isn't it? Someday when you die, they'll put one thing in the box—you. That's the tyranny of things. How much stuff can we accumulate? Coveting things leads to dishonesty, which leads to injustice, which leads to lack of relationship, because we are preoccupied with things or power or reputation.

We're all familiar with the assassination of Lincoln by John Wilkes Booth, but probably don't know the rest of the story. I read that Booth's jealousy of his brother, a well-known political figure, provoked him to pull the trigger. Here's what he's quoted as saying, "If I kill a famous person, my name will be on the front page around the world just like my brother's." He coveted a reputation and because of that, he took the life of another man, a president. The key the Bible constantly teaches us is people are more important than things. Years ago Paul Harvey reported about a lady whose husband had gotten a new car. It was just a couple of days old, and she was involved in an accident. She was so upset. The policeman said, "We've got to get your insurance number." She didn't even know where it was. She said, "It's probably in the glove compartment." She opened up the glove compartment and found the insurance card. There on the insurance card in masculine scrawl was, "I know if you're looking at this that you've had a wreck. It's OK. I love you more than I love the car." Isn't that great? What he's saying is that people are more important than things.

A survey of families showed that they estimated that all they needed was $8,000 to $11,000 more every year to be comfortable, to buy enough things. That was true no matter how much they made. If they made $15,000 they still needed $8,000 to $11,000 more. If they made $100,000 they needed $8,000 to $11,000 more. They just needed a few more things. For God's sake, guard against the passion to possess. How do you do that? We have to work on the positive. Learn to be content. Let's look at Philippians 4:11-12. Remember that Paul is not writing from a yacht out at sea, he's writing from a Roman jail. "Not that I speak in regard to need, for I have learned in whatever state I am, to be content. I know how to be abased, and I know how to abound. Everywhere and in all things I have learned both to be full and to be hungry, both to abound and to suffer need." Paul says the antidote to being a covetous person is to be a content person. The grass is always greener on the other side, but you don't know what they have to do to have green grass. They have a high water bill. They have to pay Chemlawn. They have to do all that stuff just to keep the grass greener. God says to be content with what you have. There's nothing wrong with things, but make sure your things are wings and not weights, that they allow you to do things you couldn't do otherwise, and they don't weigh you down. It's human nature to think the more we have the more content we are. Actually, the more we have, the more worried we are about taking care of it and keeping up with it. Paul says, "Learn to be content."

How do you learn to be content? You have to choose between trust and lust: whether you're going to trust God to meet your needs and give you the resources that you need or whether you're going to lust, which means to be overwhelmed and driven by self-concern, taking the short view of life. Things that gratify don't satisfy. Things are wonderful servants, but they're horrible masters. My friend, Zig Zigler, says, "You are to like the things that money can buy. There's nothing wrong with that. Like the things that money can buy, but you are to love the things that money can't buy." Family, friends, fellowship, faith — those things money cannot buy. Many people have a lot in their purse but nothing in their person; everything to live with but nothing to live for.

Learning to be content is an antidote to being covetous. But there's something that can kill covetousness. It happens when you replace the passion to possess with a passion to give, when you shoot the greedy green monster and become gracious and giving. 1 Timothy 6:17 says, "Command those who are rich in this present age not to be haughty, nor to trust in uncertain riches but in the living God, who gives us richly all things to enjoy." Enjoy those things God gives you, just hold them lightly. It's OK to own them, just don't let them own you. Verse 18, "Let them do good, that they be rich in good works, ready to give, willing to share." To share, to give, is a direct hit on the greedy green monster. It gets him off your back. You know what I've discovered? It's a whole lot better feeling to give something to someone than to make money.

It is important to look at this last commandment, because it is a hinge. Someone said that history turns on small hinges. History turns as we come to this commandment because things change.

The other commandments talked about deeds, but now we move inside. We go from deeds to desire, from action to attitude, from external to internal. We have to understand the context of the Ten Commandments. In Exodus 19, before God gives the commandments, He tells Moses to say this to the children of Israel that He brought them out of slavery, chose them, and purchased them. He didn't bring the people out because they were great and good. He brought them out because He was great and good. He didn't give these commandments because they were special. He gave them these commandments so they would be special. They are already chosen. He wanted to take those people and have them give a special gift to mankind. He wanted to use those people to touch the world. He wanted to use those people so the world would understand how great and good God was. They were chosen to do something. God has chosen each of us to do something for him. It is not because we are good but God is great and good. He has chosen us to do something special, and the moment we lose that vision and focus on ourselves, God will write "Ichabod," which means "The glory of God has departed." You can find churches all over this country which are preoccupied with themselves and look for what they can get. They forget what they were called to do — reach their city for Jesus Christ. They are dead because the glory of God has departed

The Ten Commandments were not written to make you feel guilty; they are to lead you to Christ, the positive fulfillment of those commandments. The Ten Commandments are not to take you on a guilt trip but to take you on a grace trip. The prophet Jeremiah, hundreds of years before Christ, saw Jesus coming and said that there will be a new covenant. There will be a new contract. You broke this old contract. There will be a New Testament. The New Testament will be like this: God will write this law in your mind, the mind which is in you. It's the same mind that was in Christ Jesus. God will write this commandment on your heart; it will be internal, not external. Obedience won't come from external coercion, but from internal motivation. God will come and live inside you.

John 6:27 says, "Do not labor for the food which perishes, but for the food which endures to everlasting life, which the Son of Man will give you, because God the Father has set His seal on Him." Don't give yourself to things that will end when your life ends. Concentrate on God and eternal things, so when you come to the end of your life it will be the beginning. Jesus fulfilled the Ten Commandments. Then Jesus came to give us a new way of thinking. Jesus gave us the "be" attitudes. You have to have a "be" attitude before you can have eternal behavior. It has to come from the inside out. Imposing rules from the outside creates guilt and legalism. Some of us grew up in churches with lots of do's and don'ts: you have to do this; you have to do that; you better not do this; and boy, you better not do that; and if it's fun, it has to be wrong. Jesus says it's from the inside out. You have to be connected to Him for the commandments to make sense.

Why shouldn't we covet? You were chosen, because God chose you. There's nothing special about you, but because He's great and good, He chose you. He brought you out, and because He brought you out, He wants to give you His very best. It starts with Jesus Christ. Then after that, He wants the very best life for you. Now there's another voice. There's Satan who tells us to listen to him. You have to do it yourself. You only go around once. Go for all the gusto. Get all you can. Try to be happy. Satan wants to destroy you. God wants to develop you. People who live for things are discouraged. When you live for God, life gets better and better. Some see people living for things and they look like they're doing pretty well. They have a yacht and a boat and all that kind of stuff, and they seem to be doing just fine. Well, they die. You see, it isn't over when the fat lady sings, folks. It's over when the trumpet sounds. One day when that trumpet sounds,

God will make it all right. He will straighten it all out. You don't have to worry about it. Listen to Him. Then we are thankful, grateful, contented.

We, too, were in slavery. We are a reenactment of Exodus. We were enslaved to sin. The wages of sin is death. We had no future, but God came to us just like He came to the Israelites; He came to us through His son, Jesus Christ. He is the one who delivered us. He is our Passover Lamb. He is the manna we feed on. He is our cloud by day, and He is our fire by night. He is our water that comes out of a rock. He is our Red Sea. He is our deliverer. He is the one Who comes to fulfill and do what we cannot do because the wages of sin is death. When I think about Jesus, I'm always grateful. I'm overwhelmed by how good and great He is. Why? I deserve death in hell, and I have eternal life in Heaven. That's how good God is. He wants the best for you. Why would you choose to covet someone else's plan for your life? Look to Jesus. Listen to Jesus, and you too will be satisfied and content. Having experienced overwhelming joy, you will want to share that message with other people so God receives the glory.

What has God said to you? We all struggle with this issue. If we are not careful, we look at what everyone else is borrowing and buying and we have the same mentality. We have to have more and more. We have to check our thing-o-meter to see how many things we have. The Bible says that life is not possession of a bunch of things. Life is spiritual. Life goes on for eternity. Invest in things that last.